Robert S. McGee & Dale

with *Pat Springle and Susan Joiner*

CONQUERING CHEMICAL DEPENDENCY

FACILITATOR'S GUIDE

A CHRIST-CENTERED 12-STEP PROCESS

Facilitator's Guide by Dale W McCleskey

Robert S. McGee
Publishing

ACKNOWLEDGEMENT S

Conquerin Chemical Dependencv: A Christ-Centered 12-S tev Process Facilitator's Guide
Reprint, 2000

Itern 7207-33
ISBN 978-1515029984
Dewey Decimal Number 616.8
Subject Heading: DRUG ADDICTION / DRUG ADDICTS-REHABILITATION

N ew American S tandard Bible. The Lockman Foundation, 1960, 1962, 1963, 1968, 1971, 1972, 1973, 1975, 1977. Used by permission (NASB). From the *Holy Bible, New International Version,* copyright 1973, 1978, 1984 by Interna tional Bible Society (NIV).

Printed in the United States of America

Robert S. McGee
Publishing

mcgeepubli sh ing.com | 800.460.4673

Contents

About the Author

Dale McCleskey is editor of LIFE Support Group Series materials at the LifeWay Christian Resources. He is a recovering chemical dependent and codependent with many years of participation in 12-Step groups. He was a pastor for 15 years before he joining the Adult Discipleship and Family.department at LifeWay.

Introduction

More than 15 million Americans each week are involved in some type of support group. An estimated 50,000 or more groups exist in the United States. The number of people coping with such critical life issues as divorce, chemical dependency, codependency, abuse, eating disorders, low self-esteem, and dysfunctional-family matters is escalating at a phenomenal rate. LIFE Support Series materials are designed to reach out to individuals who find themselves facing one or more of these emotional issues. LIFE Support Series materials offer the support of a Christ-centered, small-group process to bring healing and recovery in an individual's life.

Conquering Chemical Dependency: A Christ-Centered 12-Step Process and the condensed version entitled *Conquering Chemical Dependency: First Steps to a Christ-Centered 12-Step Process* both offer this type of hope. The LIFE Support Group Series resources are published because of a commitment to the ministry Jesus offered hurting people when He said:

The Spirit of the Lord is on me, because he has anointed me to preach good news to the poor. He has sent me to proclaim freedom for the prisoners and recovery of sight for the blind, to release the oppressed, to proclaim the year of the Lord's favor (Luke 4:18-19, NIV).

What is the LIFE ® Support Series?

The LIFE Support Series is an educational system of resources to help churches provide Christian ministry and emotional support for individuals in areas of social, emotional, and physical need. For purposes of understanding and training, we divide the materials into three families of groups. These three types of groups minister to different life situations and require different leadership skills. We refer to these families of groups as:
1. exploring life issues,
2. resolving life issues, and
3. taking responsibility for life issues.

In the early printings of LIFE Support Series materials you may find the terminology: *discovery group* and *support group* with the further division of three types of support group. Exploring, resolving, and taking responsibility better describes the purpose and differences between the types of groups.

1. *Exploring life issues* groups help persons to understand both themselves and others in the light of God's plan for relationships. These groups are for all people because they deal with universal human situations and because they help members learn about families and human behavior. Current examples of *Exploring* groups include: *Search for Significance, Untangling Relationships,* and *Breaking the Cycle of Hurtful Family Relationships.*

2. *Resolving Life Issues* groups lead persons through the biblical process of acceptance, forgiveness, and reconciliation in the light of God's redemptive purposes. These groups help persons who have experienced some hurt or loss to deal with the past pain that may be affecting their present lives. Examples include: *Recovering from the Losses of Life* (grief), *A Time for Healing* (divorce), *Shelter from the Storm* (sexual abuse), *Making Peace with Your Past* (painful childhood experiences), and *New Faces in the Frame* (blending a family).

3. *Taking Responsibility for Life Issues* resources lead persons through the biblical process of confession, repentance, and restitution in the light of God's redeeming power. Whereas *resolving* groups deal with past pain, *taking responsibility* groups deal with present behavior. These groups seek to help members to change deeply rooted behavior patterns and addictions. This study on chemical dependency is a *taking responsiblity* group. Other examples include *Moving Beyond Your Past, Conquering Codependency, Conquering Eating Disorders, Faithful and True* (sexual addiction), and *Quitting for Good* (nicotine addiction).

In *Conquering Chemical Dependency*, members use a Christ-centered adaptation of Alcoholics Anonymous' 12 Steps to help each other make progress in recovery from addictions. The process includes repentance, trust in God, and spiritual renewal.

The following pages will help you understand the special characteristics of the 12-Step method.

What Are the 12 Steps?

As you strive to become an effective 12-Step group facilitator, you will profit from basic understanding about the Steps. The information in this chapter will help you to answer the following questions:

- What are the 12 Steps?
- Where did they originate?
- Are the 12 Steps Christian?
- How does a Christ-centered 12-Step program differ from the secular 12-Step approach?

What Are the 12 Steps?

The 12 Steps are a process for letting God change your life—a process of repentance.

Biblical Repentance

Many believers think about repentance on a very surface level. They think that feeling sorry for our sins is repentance. Other people think that changing behavior is enough, but the biblical term for repentance means a "change of mind" as well as a change of behavior.

The Bible says that Esau, after he sold his birthright, "found no place for repentance, though he sought for it with tears" (Hebrews 12:17). That challenging verse only makes sense when you realize that repentance is a combination of God's enabling power and human-kind's choice to respond. In the fullest sense, repentance means that God restructures a person's mind. Philippians 2:12b-13 includes the balance of God's power and our cooperation. It urges: "work out your salvation with fear and trembling; for it is God who is at work in you, both to will and to work for His good pleasure." The Steps represent a structured way for a person to cooperate with God.

Here is a personal illustration. I have a number of spiritual problem areas. When someone else has something newer, better, or more expensive than I have, I sometimes experience envy. In certain situations I experience lust or greed or hatred. All of these cause me pain and difficulty. If I had the power to do so, I simply would choose or decide never to experience them again. I would give myself repentance. What is the problem with that? You know as well as I do. Try it the next time envy or greed or lust strikes. We are responsible to avoid letting these sins control our lives. However, keeping them away from our lives does not occur simply by saying, "I don't want to feel that, so I won't." Working the Steps is a way to cooperate with God while He changes our lives.

The Nature of the Steps

The **12 Steps** are a basic **set of progressive principles that make major life change possible.** Some basic methods accompany the Steps just as basic methods accompany Christianity. These practices are necessary companions to the Steps themselves. Carefully review the parts of the simple definition you just read.

The Steps are basic . They are boiled down to the simplest form. To describe the Steps one speaker used the illustration of a desert rainstorm. When the flood waters rush down a desert canyon, they wash away everything that isn't fastened down securely. After the flood only the most basic elements are left. The Steps are like that. All the unimportant things are removed. What remains are the basic principles essential for healthy, victorious living.

The Steps are progressive. They build upon each other. When we build a house, we lay the foundation before we put up the walls. In the same way the progressive nature of the Steps helps us to put first things first and to make sense of the task of living effectively. In other words we must work the Steps in order. The quality relationship with God described in Step 11 is based on giving Him your life in Step 3 and on clearing your conscience in Steps 8 and 9. You cannot make a decision to turn your life over to God in Step 3 until you have realized your own powerlessness in Step 1 and come to trust God in Step 2.

The Steps are principles. Unlike laws, principles cannot be broken. They are statements of truth like the axioms of mathematics. Under all circumstances the axiom $2 + 2 = 4$ is true. Nothing anyone can do will ever change the truth of that mathematical axiom. In the same way the Steps teach us basic principles which always will be true no matter how many people disregard them. This set of life-changing principles teaches me that I—
- cannot take God's place and manage my own life apart from Him (Step 1);

- need to come to the place in my life that I believe in and trust God (Step 2);

- need to turn control of my life over to God as I come to trust Him (Step 3).

I carry out that decision by working the remaining nine Steps (Steps 4-12). Steps 4 through 12 represent the equipment I need to carry out the decision to let God be Lord of my life. These Steps lead me to—

- become honest with myself and others about my life (Steps 4 and 5);

- allow God to change my defects of character (Steps 6 and 7);

- clear my conscience and relationships (Steps 8 and 9);

- make humility and honesty a lifestyle (Step 10);

- develop a relationship with God (Step 11);

- share this new life with others (Step 12).

The Steps also are principles we never complete fully. Like the law of gravity, which always will be in operation, the Steps are as necessary after 70 years of recovery as they are the first day.

You can see this in cooperation with the progressive nature of the Steps. We must work Step 1 before Steps 3, 7, or 11 can be effective, but we never completely finish Step 1.

Every day we are to work the Steps anew. For example, we constantly confront situations in which we must determine responsibility. We must ask the question, *Is this something which I can change, which is my business, or is this someone else's responsibility?* Every time we encounter an issue which is God's business or someone else's business, we must take Step 1 again.

In the same way we must repeat the appropriate Step in the appropriate place in our lives. This repetition is not a burden; it means that finally we have a plan of action in mind for living life effectively. The 12 Steps are a road map for a successful, effective, Christ-honoring life.

Finally, this definition says the Steps make major life change possible. A frequent slogan in the program says, "It works if you work it." The Steps don't change lives; God does. If you keep working the Steps, God will change your life.

From Where Did the Steps Come?

The Steps are not original in that someone suddenly discovered them. Since the time of Christ people have been practicing the various Steps because they are biblical principles. What is distinct about the Steps is their wording and organization. Here is an analogy: Since the days of Jesus people have been witnessing and sharing their faith. Then Bill Bright wrote a booklet called the *Four Spiritual Laws*. The booklet was not new information. It was the gospel in a more communicable, and therefore more effective, form. In the same way, the 12 Steps represent a more effective statement of truth.

In the early years of the 20th century, Lutheran evangelist Frank Buchman organized a group of believers called the Oxford Group. The Oxford Group's goals were to live a life of spiritual victory pleasing to God and to make the gospel more available to outsiders.

Group members stated six principles which they saw as essential for the victorious and effective life they were seeking. Partly as a result of the Oxford Group's ministry, a powerful spiritual conversion experience delivered Bill W., the co-founder of Alcoholics Anonymous (AA), from what was thought to be a hopeless state of alcoholism. He then became active in the Oxford Group movement. Bill W. wrote the book *Alcoholics Anonymous*. It was Bill W. who stated the Oxford Group's principles as the 12 Steps. He deleted any reference to Jesus Christ. As a compromise to reach the alienated alcoholic, he referred only to God.

Are the 12 Steps Christian?

If you are concerned about finding spiritual victory and ministering to others through the 12 Steps, you may encounter the question "Are the 12 Steps Christian?" Several possible answers exist. The principles of the Steps have a Christian heritage as described above. The Steps are truths that have a biblical origin and that have grown in their statement through history. The AA version of the Steps is not distinctively Christian, because this version deletes the identity of God. That does not mean the Steps are false or anti-Christian. They do refer to God. The personal pronouns referring to God are capitalized in the original statement of the Steps. This indicates a personal understanding of God.

Some Christians have attacked the 12 Steps, but this attack alienates those for whom Christ died. The apostle Paul chose to confront the matter in a different way. The Scripture says Paul's "spirit was being provoked within him as he was beholding the city full of idols." Rather than becoming offended and attacking the people, Paul sought to identify with them and to show them the identity of the living God. Acts 17:32 says that some listeners sneered at his message but "others said, 'We shall *hear you again concerning this.'* " By a loving approach Paul gained a hearing. As believers our evangelistic task is much more simple when we lovingly help people to see that Jesus is the God they have been seeking and that He is the ultimate source of the Steps themselves. Many Christ-centered restatements of the Steps exist. One of those is the set of Steps *Conquering Chemical Dependency* uses.

Many believers, like myself, are indebted to the program for the hope and healing they have found through the 12-Step process. The biblical principles and the strong emphasis on applying those principles has brought Christ-centered, lasting change.

The 12 Steps and the New Age

The religious beliefs of Hinduism and Buddhism have made powerful inroads in America in recent years under the guise of the New Age movement. This belief system is built on a polytheistic worldview. In this concept everything or everybody becomes God, since New Age tenets hold that the one God does not exist. The most unreasonable part of this thinking is that according to New Age concepts, individuals become god. Tragically the New Age movement has invaded much of the secular 12-Step movement. Consider the illogical nature of the situation. The person with the New Age concept of God tries to work the Steps as follows:

1. I am powerless—"but I am really god, I just don't know it."
2. I come to believe in God—"but I am god and the real God doesn't exist. What's going on here?"
3. I make a decision to turn my life and my will over to God—"but I am the only god who exists. How do I turn my will over to me?"

The Steps depend on our surrendering our life and will to the one God. New Age theology does not fit the Steps. Sadly people today are blinded, so they don't see the unreasonableness of New Age thinking.

At the heart of the New Age movement is deception. Part of the task of Christians today is to show Jesus Christ lovingly to those who have been deceived. Because they deny the objective truth, the New Agers

think that believing anything, no matter how foolish, is open-mindedness. They see Christians as prejudiced, narrow-minded bigots because the Bible teaches one God and moral absolutes. Believers need to exercise love and patience—along with clarity of thought and explanation—as they show Jesus to people.

How Does a Christ-Centered Approach Differ?

You have read an overview of the origin and nature of the Steps. You understand that both secular 12-Step programs and Christ-centered 12-Step programs exist. How do they differ? The basic, but not only, difference is the identity of God. In Christ-centered programs we recognize that our Higher Power is the Creator of the universe who reveals Himself in, and in fact is, Jesus Christ. An important difference in methodology grows out of the issue of the identity of God. Since secular groups seldom identify the specific name or character of God, the groups rely on "group consciousness" for decision-making. The highest authority in the group can be only the group itself. Christ-centered groups recognize the Word of God in written form—the Bible—as the basis of authority.

We need to observe carefully and imitate the Spirit of Jesus as we relate to our secular counterparts. Many people in secular 12-Step programs are working diligently to surrender their lives to God, but they do not know who He is. Jesus would not speak evil of or condemn these individuals as some modern believers do. What He would do—and what we must do—is love the members of these organizations and affirm the positive and biblical aspects of their program. Then we will have an opportunity to help them know the God who really lives and who loves them. The unchristlike acts of professing Christians have injured many people in secular 12-Step programs. By alienating these people further we will do nothing but shame the name of Christ.

The Methodology of the 12 Steps

We attempted to describe the nature of the 12 Steps, but a major part is missing. Christianity includes certain beliefs, but if the faith includes only these beliefs, something less than Christianity results. The genuine faith is much greater. Christianity is a relationship which includes both beliefs and actions. Likewise, the marriage relationship involves many elements including friendship, a legal commitment, and a sexual union. Any single part or group of its parts, however, does not fully define marriage. So it is with the Steps.

The 12 Steps are a set of statements, but the program includes much more than the statements. The "more" is difficult to define just as the beliefs and actions of Christianity or marriage are difficult to define. The "program" includes the Steps, the traditions, the practice of mentorship, the element of personal testimony, the group as a surrogate family, the Serenity Prayer, the slogans, and the group members supporting each other in meetings.

Mentorship or Sponsorship

An essential part of the process grows out of biblical discipleship. A strong pattern exists in Scripture for older believers guiding and discipling, sponsoring or mentoring younger disciples. Jesus made a priority out of training the twelve apostles and a smaller "inner circle" within the larger group. Paul made i t his practice to have a group of younger apprentices who spent time with him and learned from him. The apostle also gave these specific instructions for leaders to pass on what they had learned:

And the things which you have heard from me in the presence of many witnesses, these entrust to faithful men, who will be able to teach others also.

–2 Timothy 2:2

In the same way, sponsorship is a fundamental part of the 12-Step tradition. When we help a newcomer to the program through recovery, we work Step 12. In the process we are encouraged to progress in our own growth. The newcomer reminds us where we have been. The sponsor grows from the sponsoring relationship.

Encourage the newcomer to watch the lives of the participants and to find a person who shows   evidence of growth in his or her life. An important goal for a group is to provide a list of quality sponsors. The newcomer enlists a sponsor who then supervises the newcomer in his or her growth.

Everyone needs a mentor or sponsor. Many excellent Christian leaders for years have taught that anyone who seeks to be a Christian leader needs to learn from a more mature leader, and everyone needs to share his or her discipleship with someone. Be aware that the newcomer may need special encouragement to find a sponsor because this is a critical element in working the Steps.

Step Work

"Step Work" refers to the process of doing the writing, taking the inventories, and performing the actions the 12 Steps call for. Step work is the other side of sponsorship and is the discipleship process through which the sponsor leads the newcomer. This first-person story shows the relationship of sponsorship and Step work:

When I f irst entered recovery, someone told me plainly, "This program only works if you get a sponsor and do the Step work." I didn't know a sponsor from a chimpanzee or Step work from corned beef, but I did know that I was in pain and that these were people who cared and whose lives showed evidence of recovery. I looked at the sponsor list, walked up to one of the "old timers" in the group, and said: "Will you be my sponsor?" During the next few months my sponsor became one of my dearest friends. My sponsor gave me written assignments to complete. *Conquering Chemical Dependency: A Christ-Centered 12-Step Process* and *Conquering Chemical Dependency: First Steps to a Christ-Centered 12-Step Process* now are available for this purpose. As we met, I talked through my work. The year I spent working with my sponsor was the most liberating and healing experience in many years. The healing was part of and was surpassed only by my salvation experience.

In the years that followed I have served as a sponsor for many others in recovery. I have received much healing as I have continued this process. The joy of leading someone to Jesus and then helping that person grow is paralleled by the joy of helping someone gain recovery and begin to live an effective, Christ-honoring life. The icing on the cake is watching as this person passes the process along to others. The Scripture says, "Cast your bread on the surface of the waters, for you will find it after many days" (Ecclesiastes 11:1). This verse is fulfilled over and over again in recovery groups. People begin to give themselves away, and the process comes back to them in a multitude of wonderful ways.

The *Big Book* (*Alcoholics Anonymous*) gives basic instruction in how to do Step work. As the 12-Step program has grown and has been applied to more problems, the guides available to do Step work also have grown. *Conquering Chemical Dependency* and *First Steps* are designed for use in the Step work process with a sponsor. The plan is very simple. The newcomer enlists a sponsor and acquires a copy of *Conquering Chemical Dependency* or *First Steps*; then the newcomer does the work and shares the material with his or her sponsor. Of all the ways to use the book, working the material one on one with a sponsor, along with attending a support group, will prove the most effective in creating lasting change.

The Slogans

The recovery movement has produced several slogans which are informal restatements of the key concepts of the Steps themselves. Making an exhaustive list of the slogans is impossible, but we can recognize that the slogans mean much to those who struggle with issues which often are overwhelming. Some of the slogans include: *Let Go and Let God, Easy Does It, Discovery Is Not Recovery, People Make Mistakes—People Aren't Mistakes,* and many more. Many of these are found in the margins of the member's book.

Slogans are important because they communicate practical truth in ways that people can understand and apply. In fact, new slogans are born each time another person applies the truth to his or her life. The slogan *Live Life on Life's Terms* seems to be nonsense until its meaning hits home. We frequently refuse to deal with issues on the basis of reality. We attempt to live in a dream world in which things are as we wish they were, or we live with the specter of how we fear things might become. *Live Life on Life's Terms* calls us to objectivity. We must live with what is real.

The Serenity Prayer

The Serenity Prayer is so closely linked with the 12-Step recovery process, it almost is inseparable. The prayer summarizes the Steps themselves. People repeat the prayer in countless meetings every day. (See page 196 in the member's book for a copy of the Serenity Prayer.)

Chemical dependency stems from issues related to control. We have experienced circumstances which feel out of control. We found that the mood-altering substances were a way to regain the feeling of control. In our attempt to feel in control, we displaced God and attempted to take His place.

The Serenity Prayer is an appeal for a specific solution for the compulsive, controlling addict. The Serenity Prayer asks for the peace necessary to stop trying to control things which are none of our business. While a person compulsively controls, he or she also leaves much undone. When someone tries to control all people and circumstances which are not his or her business, neither time nor energy remains to tend to responsibilities. The typical result is a family or relationship in which everyone is controlling and manipulating each other and no one is tending to his or her own responsibilities. Praying the Serenity Prayer involves asking God for the courage for us to be responsible for our own business.

The Traditions

The 12 Traditions are the companions to the 12 Steps. Your Christ-centered 12-Step program may want to use the traditions in some form. We provide for you the *Conquering Chemical Dependency* Principles[1] on page 63. These involve a Christ-centered restatement of the principles in the 12 Traditions. Facilitators will benefit from becoming familiar with the 12 Traditions of Alcoholics Anonymous. Since the 12 Traditions have been the guiding polity of most 12-Step groups, the traditions are very important to many of those you may desire to reach. On page 61 of this guide we have printed the 12 Traditions. Anyone who wants to be knowledgeable about the movement will profit by reading the book *Twelve Steps and Twelve Traditions,* published by AA World Services, the standard reference to the Steps and the Traditions.

Notes

[1]Adapted from *Right Step Facilitator Training Manual* (Houston: Rapha Publishing, 1990).

Foundational Concepts

A Christ-centered 12-Step group is not a typical Bible study in which the lecture method is the primary teaching vehicle. In fact, many of your church's best Bible teachers may not be qualified to lead a support group because they might not possess some of the important skills listed below. The support-group facilitator guides the group process, allows group members to share information and insights, and assists members ready to identify and explore their own feelings about certain issues the sharing prompts.

Since shared leadership is a part of the 12-Step tradition, think in terms of three levels or stages of leadership in groups.
• Every group needs at least one facilitator. The facilitator is the liaison person, responsible to the church.
• A co-facilitator is a facilitator in training. The co-facilitator also can be in charge when the facilitator cannot be present for a group session.
• Persons in the group who are working their Steps will learn to introduce a topic and to begin the sharing for meetings. Sponsors can help those they sponsor to know when they are ready to begin to lead meetings.

By using this three-stage leadership development plan your group will accomplish two important tasks. You will develop facilitators and leaders, and you will avoid the problem of immature and unhealthy leadership.

Important spiritual qualifications for a support-group facilitator are to—

• be a Christian with a growing personal relationship with Jesus Christ;
• be a person of prayer and daily Bible study;
• be an active member of a local church;
• have a sense of God's call to the ministry of support groups;
• be spiritually gifted for the work;
• have a commitment to confidentiality within the group;
• be willing to give time and energy to help group members;
• have a teachable spirit;
• be sensitive to the daily leadership of the Holy Spirit;
• love the Lord and love people.

One specialized qualification exists for facilitators of Christ-centered 12-Step groups. The facilitator must be a person who is working the 12 Steps in his or her own life. Facilitators need to have been in recovery from chemical dependency for at least two years. Do not attempt to facilitate or to lead a group without being on a recovery journey—with accountability to someone in a sponsor relationship. In some cases those beginning a 12-Step group form a "buddy system" to work their Steps. The key is to be working the Steps with accountability to another person.

People who have led groups through *MasterLife*, *Disciple's Prayer Life*, or *Experiencing God* have a strong spiritual foundation for leading support groups. *LIFE Support Leader's Handbook* (item 7268-02) and *Wise Counsel: Skills for Lay Counseling* (item 7259-08) are strongly recommended as resources for potential support-group leaders.

The numbered paragraphs which follow discuss important interpersonal qualifications for a support-group facilitator. As you read them, you may feel overwhelmed at the range of skills this book suggests for a support-group facilitator.

I suspect you are reading this facilitator's guide precisely because you've sensed a calling to meet the deeply felt needs of people. If you are interested in facilitating a group like this, I encourage you to talk to your support-group coordinator, pastor, or sponsor to see what kinds of training and experience you need and whether the timing is right for you to facilitate such a group. Your support-group coordinator or pastor can provide honest, encouraging, helpful feedback about whether this is a wise step for you at this point in your life.

1. Be an effective communicator in sending messages. Communication involves both verbal and nonverbal skills. The set of your mouth, the look in your eyes, and the tone of your voice all communicate to group members the message you are sending. Those who study communication tell us—
• only 7 percent of any message is contained in the words the person speaks;
• 38 percent of any message is contained in the tone of voice the person uses;
• 55 percent of any message is contained in the nonverbal cues surrounding a person's words.

Communication experts further tell us that when the verbal message and the nonverbal message clash, the nonverbal message is the one people believe! Intuitively, you know this is true. Ever asked a jaw-clenched, arms-crossed, red-in-the-face person, "Anything wrong?" and heard in reply, "Nothing; I'm fine. Why do you ask?" Moments like these are almost comical. Whether or not your discussion continued, you knew this person and that moment in his life was anything but fine.

Sometimes your role as effective message sender involves repeating what you hear group members say. Comments like: "What I hear you saying is . . ." or "Help me understand what you're telling us; are you saying . . . ?" allow you and that group member to communicate accurately during group sessions.

2. Be an effective listener who knows how to hear meanings and not just words. Your group members will be dealing with critical life issues; they frequently feel a desperate need for someone to hear their story and to understand their pain. Listening is a skill everyone can practice and develop.

Give group members undivided attention when they speak. Keep your eyes focused on the individual speaking. Prevent interruptions to help other group members respect the one speaking. An especially important thing to remember is to resist the urge to plan your next words while someone speaks.

Occasionally a good listener gives nonverbal feedback—raised eyebrows, nod of the head, a smile, or a sympathetic groan. He may lean forward in a chair, with his arms and hands relaxed and uncrossed—and give verbal feedback—"I understand," "Please continue," "I know that feeling well."

You may be shocked occasionally by information some group members disclose. Your role is not to communicate judgment or censure or to reinterpret their experiences. Be careful; your nonverbal cues often communicate these attitudes, even if your words do not. Your role is to create a safe place for disclosure and to create a confidential setting in which honesty is the first step toward recovery and healing.

3. Be a servant leader in the group. A support-group leader must be a companion-traveler with group members traveling the road of recovery and spiritual growth. However, the group leader also is a traveler who has been on the road longer and who can help interpret the road's markers. Group members need to know that their leader empathetically identifies with

their struggles to change and still is in the process of change, too.

Most importantly, offer your history and your hope as Jesus did. Jesus was a servant leader who the Scriptures tell us was willing to wash the feet of others. When you share your own struggles, listen to a fifth Step, or help a newcomer to understand and work the program, you will be filling this function for your support-group members by demonstrating a servant spirit.

4. Be an encourager to each group member. Encouragement is essential to the group process. During group sessions provide continual encouragement to individual members and to the group itself.

No matter what happens during the group's time together, find a way to affirm or encourage its members. Some members may give the group only their presence for weeks; affirm the courage required of them to keep attending. Some members will be able to tell their stories only with tears; affirm the courage to be honest in the presence of other people.

5. Be skilled in preventing one person from dominating the group. As you prevent one from dominating the group, understand why she is doing so. More than likely, she's never felt a safe place or an appropriate time to admit to her wounds or describe her pain. The group provides these key elements to healing. Some people will rush toward this experience like a dammed-up river finally released rushes downstream. When a group member finally tells something she's never told, let the story flow until the powerful rushing of words begins to calm and slow.

One person's dominating can damage the group. Sometimes a gentle interruption which summarizes what the monopolizer has said brings the monologue to a halt. Occasionally you'll need to restate the topic of the meeting; this reinvites the rest of the group to respond. Sometimes, with gentle humor, you'll say: "Joe, you've convinced us how strongly you feel about this! Let's see if another member has an experience or feeling he or she would like to share." You may need to talk to the person outside the group about his or her domination of the group discussion time.

6. Know how to be involved personally without relinquishing leadership. From the time of the first meeting never forget the importance of the group members' seeing you as a fellow struggler. Without dominating, allow the group to know you as one who has faults, failures, and fears about relationships in your life.

7. Know how to keep all group members involved in the group's life and process. Remember, you've already noted that lecture is inappropriate for support groups. If you are comfortable using only the lecture method, do not attempt to lead a support group. This group employs a process of sharing. It needs the involvement of every group member.

Let group sessions build on the significant work group members do between sessions in their *Conquering Chemical Dependency* members' books. However, allowing members to share freely is far more important than is sticking legalistically to a group session plan you develop before the session begins. Group members sometimes arrive at the session absolutely bursting at the seams to share something that happened in their lives during the past week that relates to their Step work. Be sensitive to this tendency and be flexible. Many of the best meetings will just happen as group members share something unrelated to the topic you have chosen.

Do not criticize group members for the feelings and insights they share, especially when you find yourself disagreeing with them. In the same way do not allow other group members to criticize one another. If they do, trust in the group and concern for its members never will develop.

8. Know how and when to refer persons for professional help. Be sure your referral strategy is in place before you conduct the first group session. With your pastor or another staff member's help, identify appropriate professional counselors and agencies in your vicinity. If possible talk ahead of time to your referral sources about the specific types of services they offer and about such matters as costs, availability, and emergency service.

As the group progresses, certain members may need professional Christian counseling. Be sensitive to needs for additional help at places where group members have a strong emotional response to needs. During group sessions do not suggest to group members that they need counseling, but speak individually and privately with group members who you believe need this level of care. Share with the group member your impressions about his or her need for more than the group is able to offer, and help him or her make referral choices. The *LIFE Support Leader's Handbook* and the LIFE course *WiseCounsel: Skills for Lay Counseling* contain units dealing with how to refer persons.

9. Know how to integrate biblical and psychological truth. It can be done! When psychological truth is

based on biblical truth, we obtain clear insight into how the human mind, body, and spirit function. One example of a psychological concept explained in a biblical reference is: "For as he [a man] thinks within himself, so he is" (Proverbs 23:7, NASB).

Follow this simple rule: Be sure psychological precepts have a scriptural/biblical base. At the same time don't allow group members to deny emotional and behavioral problems by coloring these problems with religious phrases. Group discussions can integrate as one concept the biblical and psychological approaches to human needs. You do not need two separate discussions on each issue.

10. Expect the unexpected! You'll never be able to control every eventuality in planning for group sessions. You won't have that kind of prophetic insight! Expecting the unexpected is your way to commit yourself to the leading of the Holy Spirit.

Plan well each week, but do not adhere to your plans so rigidly that you cannot recognize what God is doing in the group. Moment by moment you must "lean not on your own understanding" (Proverbs 3:5, NIV) so that you can trust the leadership of the Holy Spirit.

Interpersonal Qualifications for a Support-Group Leader

1. Be an effective communicator in sending messages.
2. Be an effective listener who knows how to hear meanings, not just words.
3. Be a servant leader in the group.
4. Be an encourager to each group member.
5. Be skilled in preventing one person from dominating the group.
6. Know how to be involved personally without relinquishing leadership.
7. Know how to keep all group members involved in the group's life and process.
8. Know how and when to refer people for professional help.
9. Know how to integrate biblical and psychological truth.
10. Expect the unexpected!

Choose a Schedule and a Plan

When you hear the term *12-Step group,* several images may come to mind, because a variety of types of groups exist. Three general types of groups in the recovery tradition are: the speaker's meeting, the Step-study meeting, and the sharing meeting. Certain customary preliminaries to the meeting are common in most groups. These preliminaries include:

1. Welcome and reading of the group preamble, which describes the nature and purpose of the particular group.
2. Reading of the Steps and/or Traditions.
3. Reminder of confidentiality.
4. Prayer, most often the Serenity Prayer and the Model Prayer (also called the Lord's Prayer).
5. The "seventh tradition"—a freewill offering to maintain the group's self-supporting status. (See the 12 Traditions on page 62.)
6. Hugs, which are an important part of the affirmation members give each other.

A **speaker's meeting** is one in which an individual presents a testimony about his or her own recovery experiences. The speaker may be the facilitator, someone who has volunteered, or perhaps a person someone has invited to share with the group. As the name implies, the speaker's meeting is the type having the least amount of group participation. The speaker's meeting is more common in the Alcoholics Anonymous (AA) tradition than in other types of groups. This type of meeting is particularly valuable for introducing the newcomer to the program. Some groups may find i t effective to have a monthly speaker's meeting with a sharing or Step-study meeting on the other weeks.

Step-study meetings come in a great many shapes and descriptions. The common element of Step-study meetings is a format for studying and applying the 12 Steps. Some Step-study meetings are as basic as listening to cassette recordings and then taking time for personal writing or journaling. Other Step-study meetings are organized around reading and discussion of a book.

Conquering Chemical Dependency and *First Steps* are written to be used effectively in a Step-study meeting. AA groups often have Step-study meetings based on the study of the "12 and 12" (*The 12 Steps and 12 Traditions*), which is a text for anyone interested in learning more about the AA model of the Steps.

The third approach is the **sharing meeting** . In this format the facilitator or a mature group member usually introduces the topic for the meeting and the members share how the particular topic applies to their recovery. Sharing meetings have been called "feelings" meetings because they help participants get in touch with their emotions. The topics for this type of meeting can be determined by a set course of study or determined by the leaders from week to week.

Group members can lead the meetings in a very unstructured way or in a more restricted fashion. Those who lead meetings should be those who have progressed in their recovery and working the Steps.

While sharing meetings probably are the most useful meetings, be aware of one guideline. Keep the group's focus on the 12 Steps, God's Word, and recovery. Keep meetings from becoming focused only on the pain of the past or a recital of past actions. Healthy meetings do not neglect the past or the pain, but they move toward change and growth.

Why This Overview?

I have given you this overview to prepare you for several scenarios you probably will encounter in group l ife. One is the "this-group-isn't-doing-it-right" episode. Remember that we who suffer addictions are controllers. At some time in the ministry of groups you will encounter a highly controlling person who will announce that the group is doing things all wrong. No single right way to do a 12-Step group exists. Focusing on purpose is much more effective than is doing it "right" or "perfectly." Prepare your group ministry so that the type or types of meetings are appropriate and are meeting needs.

A second reason for understanding something about the history and types of groups is a leadership issue. The 12-Step tradition is one of lay leadership. The second tradition of AA states that "for our group purpose there is but one ultimate authority—a loving God as He may express Himself in our group conscience. Our leaders are but trusted servants; they do not govern."[1]

Avoid two extremes in determining the type of leadership for your group. The first extreme is conducting   a class instead of a group. Leaders must avoid exercising excessive control. Group members grow as they help each other. They need to have opportunity to share the leadership. The other extreme to avoid is a lack of leadership. Many times the sickest member of the group will be eager to control the group, fix everyone else, and give out advice in all directions. The skill of a facilitator is to avoid dominating while maintaining enough group leadership to keep someone else from dominating the group.

Choose a Schedule and Plan

Several options exist for the schedule and calendar plan of a 12-Step recovery group. The issues in choosing an approach include the duration or term for a group, the plan for covering the content of the Steps, and whether to have an open or closed group.

Length of Term for a Group

Groups in the 12-Step tradition generally are ongoing, open-ended groups. Other options also exist for 12-Step groups. Here are three general approaches. Consider prayerfully the advantages and disadvantages of each.

Option 1: The Ongoing Group

Ongoing groups with no ending date represent the first option. This option has the advantage of long-term consistency. The group always is there when people have a need. In time the group becomes known to the community so that a network of referrals can develop. The method also has a weakness. The method fits the chemical dependent person's inclination to procrastinate. If the group does not schedule an ending date, the member will not have an ultimate goal to work toward.

Option 2: Ongoing Group with Specific Term

A specific term for a group provides an incentive to work the Steps. The fact that the group has a beginning and ending date encourages one to complete his or her Step-work.

We suggest three options for specific terms of moderate length. You can adapt the approach to your situation and needs from these models. The first is a "school-year" model. Form the group in the fall—August or September—and continue it through the spring—April or May. The other possibilities are groups having one-year or two-year terms. In all cases

you can reorganize the groups for another term for those who have incomplete work or for those who wish to continue to grow and minister through a 12-Step group.

A second advantage of groups with a specific term with a beginning and ending date is a matter of leadership. A church can enlist leadership more easily for a specific term.

Option 3: The Step-Study Group Model

A group can be very valuable on a shorter term and more specifically on a Step-study plan. The simplest expression of this model would be a 12-week study to cover the 12 Steps. A 24-week format will allow more time to deal with each Step. If the group uses a study format, this format can be an introduction to the Steps. The facilitator needs to explain clearly to members that much more time than 12 weeks is necessary to process the material thoroughly. In a 12-week setting, the group takes the form of a discovery group on the Steps for the purpose of understanding and providing a general overview of the Steps. This 12-week model does not allow time genuinely to work the Steps, but it does provide opportunities for members to become familiar with the process.

Remember, the 12-Step tradition is broad and flexible. In 12-Step groups, as in churches, some people will think only one option exists. Be prepared for an inevitable occurrence. Someone who has joined from another group will think the group should operate differently. Precedent exists for each of the models mentioned above. For example, some treatment centers traditionally have required people to complete a predetermined number of the Steps before the patient is discharged.

Prayerfully select the approach with the advantages to meet your need and the disadvantages with which you can live. Then trust the Holy Spirit to work through the process. The process really does "work when you work it."

Open or Closed Groups?

Jargon is specialized language a specific group of people use. Computer programmers, photographers, mechanics, and other groups have their own jargon. The following is an example of how jargon can cause misunderstanding:

At a chemical dependency conference a social worker repeatedly used the word *enabler*, which he meant as a

1

positive term. Using the jargon of his field, he used enabler to refer to someone who helps people by empowering them to get the services they need. His audience had a specialized language with which he was not acquainted. For them the term *enabler* had a bad connotation. It meant one who takes responsibility for an irresponsible person and so adds to the problem. This speaker failed to communicate because he didn't understand the jargon.

Become aware of specialized terms. Watch out for the misunderstanding they can cause.

Open meeting and *closed* meeting have different meanings in the 12-Step tradition than they do in other types of groups. In other LIFE Support Group Series groups, closed means the group has a specific number of participants who began the group together; the group does not permit new group members after the second or third meeting. In the 12-Step tradition *closed* normally means a group which only permits those recovering from the specific problem. A closed AA group only permits alcoholics. But such a closed group is not closed to new participants.

Distinguish four types of open/closed groups:
- completely open groups (ongoing groups open to individuals whether or not they are chemically dependent)
- limited time frame (closed schedule) open groups (open to all people)
- ongoing (no scheduled ending date) closed groups (for chemically dependent people only)
- completely closed groups (limited time frame, for chemically dependent individuals only)

Each group has its own distinct advantages. A completely closed group builds greater trust and confidentiality. A closed group which permits only people recovering from a specific issue such as chemical dependency but which permits new members to join the group sometimes is appropriate. Similarly open groups sometimes are best. Understand the options and clearly communicate the intent of the group.

An advantage of open membership is that such groups allow seekers to participate to see if the group meets their needs. Some people come to a group asking themselves if they have a problem. Hearing the stories of others helps them to assess their own situation.

An advantage of open-schedule groups is availability. The group is available when a person senses his or her need. No need exists to wait until a new group begins.

Balance: Urgency Versus Controlling

We who minister to chemical dependents must find the difficult balance between doing all we can for another person and allowing that person to face his or her own responsibility. We may need to use every device at our disposal to intervene in the situation. At other times we must back off and say, "I love you, but if you insist on being stupid, it is your decision. I'll be here when you finally become willing to face the truth."

If you have an open group, be prepared for one possibly troubling result. Many people will drift into and out of the group. If you or other leaders feel that you must retain every group member, you will be in for much anxiety. Learn to let the Holy Spirit work in people's lives. People require time to see themselves objectively. Allow them the time they need. If you are involved for several years in 12-Step ministry, you will see people attend, drop out after a few meetings, and then later return to work the program seriously.

Many people have so much denial, have damaged themselves so seriously, or are so deeply hurt that healing for them is a long, slow process. The ongoing, open group can accommodate the person who requires a year of meetings to develop enough trust and insight to begin the recovery journey.

Remember, no single schedule or plan is best for all situations. Before it begins a group, the church can make some purposeful decisions about each of these issues. Develop newcomer materials that will clearly communicate the nature and purpose of the group.

Using the Newcomer's Packet

Prepare a packet of materials to give newcomers who attend open groups. The newcomer's material will explain the nature, purpose, and procedures of the group. You will find a sample newcomer's pack on pages 58-59. You may copy or adapt the sample to use in your group. For the newcomer's material you also can copy the Christ-centered 12-Steps and the *Conquering Chemical Dependency* principles from pages 62-63. Add to the packet whatever information you consider important about meeting times and additional church services. Seek to answer the questions the new group member might ask. Well-prepared newcomer materials are a great asset to your group ministry.

Notes
[1] Alcoholics Anonymous World Services, Inc., New York, New York.

How to Begin a 12-Step Group

Actions for Starting a Group

The following actions can help you prepare to minister effectively through a 12-Step recovery group. If you are the pastor, minister of education, or person in charge of recovery groups, these specific actions will give you a checklist to prepare for beginning a new group. In the *LIFE Support Leader's Handbook* (item 7268-02) you will find additional helps for administrating a group ministry.

If you are preparing to facilitate a 12-Step group, this checklist will help you in your preparation. Since the checklist is written for this dual purpose, disregard actions such as selecting the group's facilitator that already have been completed.

✎ **Check each of the following steps as you complete them:**

❏ Pray
❏ Select the group's facilitator
❏ Enlist a co-facilitator
❏ Understand foundational concepts for all types of recovery groups
❏ Determine the logistics
❏ Order materials
❏ Set fees
❏ Determine child-care arrangements
❏ Promote the group
❏ Get started

Action 1: Pray

Prayer is the essential ingredient for any ministry in the church. God honors individuals who seek after Him. God already has begun to use LIFE Support Group Series ministries through the care of local churches to work in the lives of hurting people.

Once your church arrives at a sense of calling and a time of decision about providing support-group ministries, your church will be accepting God's invitation to join Him in a work He already is doing.

Support-group leaders likely will feel the need to pray each week for their group members and for their specific needs. Use prayer to begin your personal study time and your preparation time for the group sessions.

You can use the opportunity of facilitating this group to learn about the power and presence of God through your own personal prayer pilgrimage.

Action 2: Select the group's facilitator

Study carefully on pages 21-23 of this guide the section on leading a *Conquering Chemical Dependency* 12-Step group. Consider the spiritual and interpersonal skills these pages discuss. Suggest that those people in your church who select group facilitators use this information while they make these decisions. The skills for being a group facilitator differ from the skills for some types of teaching.

You also would find this same information useful in the hands of prospective group facilitators and sponsors. Encourage them to study this information prayerfully as they seek an answer to the invitation to lead meetings or to sponsor others.

Twelve-Step groups are uniquely confessional. Facilitators do not teach; they share their own journey. Pray for and select facilitators who are recovering from chemical dependency—who will be able to share their experience in recovery. As you read the group leadership models, you will see that a concerned person who is not in recovery will not be able to lead effectively.

Action 3: Enlist a co-facilitator

Begin now to pray for those members in each 12-Step group who are capable of leading meetings. During group sessions look for these individuals. As they gain the necessary experience—particularly as they actively work their Steps—they will become capable of leading meetings.

Action 4: Determine the logistics

A 12-Step group may meet at any time that fits the church's schedule and that meets the needs of the people. People in your group need anonymity. Consider scheduling your group's sessions during a time the church is free of all other activities. Arrange for the group to meet in the same place each week and in a location away from the normal flow of other church activity. Select a distraction-free setting which will not hinder sharing among group members. Look for comfortable, movable furniture, and check on adequate lighting, heating, and cooling of the room. Establish a clearly understood starting time. As a group plan to negotiate about ending time. The minimum amount of time is one hour to one and a half hours. Page 20 contains suggested formats.

Action 5: Order materials

Order sufficient copies of the following materials well in advance of your first meeting:

• *Conquering Chemical Dependency: A Christ-Centered 12-Step Process* (item 7206-33; ISBN 0-8054-9983-0) or *Conquering Chemical Dependency: First Steps to a Christ-Centered 12-Step Process* (item 7213-94; ISBN 0-8054-9972-5), one for each group member, facilitator, and co-facilitator. Keep copies of the book on hand for newcomers to purchase as they join the group. *First Steps* is the 64-page version of the larger 224-page workbook. *First Steps* is a good choice for someone who has had limited time in recovery or has limited reading skills. Both workbooks may be used at the same time by individuals in the same group.

• *Conquering Chemical Dependency: A Christ-Centered 12-Step Process Facilitator's Guide* (item 7207-33; ISBN 0-8054-9984-9), one guide for each facilitator and co-facilitator. Provide copies of the guide for those who begin to lead meetings and for those who serve as sponsors.

You can buy these resources at local LifeWay Christian Stores, contact Customer Service Center, MSN 113, 127 Ninth Avenue, North; Nashville, TN 37234-0113; FAX (615) 251-5933; or email *customerservice@lifeway.com*.

Action 6: Set fees

Christ-centered 12-Step groups charge no fees. In keeping with the seventh tradition, the group is self supporting through its own contributions. At each meeting groups pass a collection basket. Groups may use contributions to pay for child care (if your church does not provide it free), to pay for refreshments, or to pay for books and materials. Typically, the group members pay the cost of their books. Your church may want to provide partial scholarships for those who cannot afford a member's book. Even if your church subsidizes a portion of the cost of the books, asking the members to pay something for their workbooks still is

important because —
• it immediately establishes a level of commitment of time and resources to join the group;
• it allows group members to feel they are contributing something to the support-group ministry.

However, do not use fees to pay the group's facilitator. Christ-centered support groups are lay-led, not professionally-led, groups. This important detail will help protect your church from legal liability.

Action 7: Determine child-care arrangements

Decide before you begin promoting the group whether your church will offer child care for group members' children. Such a service is essential for some people to join your group. Certainly the cost of child care is important to consider.

Sometimes group sessions do not wrap up neatly at the same time each week. This is difficult for children and child-care providers alike.

Action 8: Promote the group

Schedule at least a three-week period for promoting the group. Here is a suggested method for determining what group to begin and for promoting the new group.

❑ Determine in a preliminary way the need you wish the group to meet. You probably will do this by brainstorming ideas or simply by accepting some-one's proposal. Carefully note the word *preliminary*. This is what you *think* the need is. If you proceed on the basis of your unverified idea, you may be very disappointed in the result.
❑ Plan a public informational meeting. If you think you need to begin a chemical dependency group, you might ask a speaker from your church or from some other organization to speak on a topic related to chemical dependency. Publicize the meeting as being strictly informational. People are not required to make a commitment in order to attend.
❑ Conduct the information meeting and take a survey. Provide a survey sheet for participants to state in what, if any, group they would be interested. Provide a wide range of topics such as chemical dependency, grief, divorce, eating disorders, weight loss, or recovery from sexual abuse.
❑ From the responses you receive at the meeting determine the genuine need. Now you are not oper-ating on what you *think* the need might be. Now you are operating on concrete responses.

❑ Follow the action plans in this guide and in the *LIFE Support Leader's Handbook* to provide the necessary leaders, materials, and place to begin the group or groups.

❑ Publicize the group in ways you consider appropriate, and begin.

Since 12-Step groups are anonymous, be very careful about registration. Recording participants by first name only is an option. The only requirement for membership in a 12-Step group is the desire to recover. Be careful not to make registration an obstacle to participation. The group can keep and periodically update a phone list. Discourage any attempt at formal record keeping. If someone asks the leader of a support group how many people attended his or her group, the leader can give a stock answer to satisfy the inquirer.

Determine your target audience. If you plan to target only church members, then use your church's normal channels of promotion, such as the church's newsletter, posters, or bulletin inserts. Your pastor could preach one or several sermons from Luke 4:18-19, which describes Jesus' healing ministry. Chapter 1 of the *LIFE Support Leader's Handbook* provides a sample sermon. If the pastor supports a LIFE Support Group Series ministry, members of the congregation will see groups as an extension of Jesus' ministry to hurting people.

If you plan an enlistment campaign outside your church, then promote the group by using free publicity like public-service announcements or notices on your newspaper's religion page. Your church can print posters inexpensively and can ask church members to post these notices in their places of business. A church can use a small card or brochure about support groups as part of the visitor's packet or during outreach visits in homes. Many churches have found a support-group ministry to be an effective outreach option. One church grew from 200 to 5,000 members because of its effective recovery ministry.

Chapter 3 of the *LIFE Support Leader's Handbook* offers many suggestions for promoting LIFE Support Group Series courses inside and outside the church. Designate someone in the church office to deal with inquiries about groups. Make certain the person designated is knowledgeable about the subject. All publicity, in or outside the church, can list a phone number to call for more information.

Action 9: Get started

Review the eight actions in this overview to ensure you have covered all necessary details. Ideally, you will

have worked the Steps before you begin a new group. If you are beginning a new ministry and you have no means to work the Steps before you begin the group, familiarize yourself with the first three units in the member's book and with the facilitator's guide. This will help you become familiar with the Steps. Read the facilitator's guide sections entitled "What Are the Steps?", "Foundational Concepts," and "Choose a Schedule and a Format," as well as this unit on how to lead meetings. Schedule a meeting with your co-facilitator to review details. Study together the first unit in the member's book and facilitator's guide, and plan your first group session.

As you look at the group leadership models on pages 27-49, remember the distinctive of 12-Step meetings. Do not use all the models in each meeting. Select a single topic, then briefly explain it. Share how the topic impacts your life. Invite the group members to share how the topic impacts their lives. Each person is free to pass if he or she does not wish to share. Each person shares only about his or her own issues. If you are conducting a Step-study group or a short-term introduction to the 12 Steps, you will find more help at the first of each Step in the group leadership models that begin on page 27.

The introductory meeting for a new group is the time to introduce people to the distinctives of the 12-Step format. If possible, place in a new group people with experience in the Steps. In some cases those experienced persons will not be available. The group members will mature in the process together.

You probably will find yourself steering the group away from cross-talk and advice-giving. Cross-talk occurs when individuals speak out of turn and interrupt each other. Don't be discouraged. Learning to respect other people's boundaries takes time.

The introductory meeting is a good time to distribute members' books and to introduce participants to the LIFE Support Group Series course format. Emphasize that actually doing the written work and sharing it with a sponsor when possible is vital to recovery. You also may choose to provide a brief overview of the Steps as participants look through their members' books and as you explain the course map on the inside back cover of their books. (Highlighting with members the unit page for each Step provides a good summary of each Step's content.) The abbreviated format of *First Steps* does not include the course map or unit pages. With *First Steps* you simply may overview the four- to six-page units covering each Step.

Meeting Formats

Select the meeting format to fit your group and time frame. The options include a traditional format, an additional Bible study option, a short-term Step-study format, or any number of variations to fit your situation.

Traditional Format

1. Quiet moment (1 min.)
2. Read opening group remarks and prayer (1 min.)
3. Read Christ-centered 12 Steps, page 62 (3 min.). Read the *Conquering Chemical Dependency* Principles, page 63. (optional)
4. Welcome new members and guests. Ask new members to introduce themselves by first name if they wish (3-10 min.)
5. Introduce facilitator or speaker for the group (2 min.)
6. Pass the collection and prayer basket (1 min.)
7. Content for the week (45-60 min.)
8. Read "Declaration," page 59 (1 min.)
9. Close with the Lord's Prayer or the Serenity Prayer (1 min.)

Optional Format with Bible-Study Time

1. Read opening group remarks and prayer (1 min.)
2. Read Christ-centered 12 Steps, page 62 (1 min.) Read the *Conquering Chemical Dependency* Principles, page 63. (optional)
3. Welcome new members and guests. Ask new members to introduce themselves by first name if they wish (3-10 min.)
4. Introduce facilitator or speaker for the group (2 min.)
5. Pass the collection and prayer basket (1 min.)
6. Sharing (30-45 min.)
7. Bible study (30 min.)
7. Read "Declaration," page 59 (1 min.)
8. Close with prayer (1 min.)

One approach to Bible study is to ask a person to lead the study as you would with any other Bible study. Another approach is to assign each group member who desires to read a Scripture from the list of Scriptures in the facilitator's guide.

Allow the group members a few moments to read and to think about their assigned Scriptures. Then allow members to read their assigned passages and to make whatever application of them they desire. To avoid doctrinal conflict, allow comment only from the person to whom you've assigned the Scripture. Do not allow others to add their comments.

Groups also can adapt the Bible-study format to a Step study. During the Step-study time you can study one or more lessons from *Conquering Chemical Dependency*. Consider reversing the order by scheduling the Bible study or Step study before the sharing time. If the study time precedes the sharing, then the sharing can be related to the Bible or Step study. Similarly, if the sharing is first, then you can do the Bible or Step study related to the topic of sharing.

Short-Term Step-Study Format

Groups can adapt the 12-Step meeting to a study of the Steps in a limited time frame. One caution is in order. Make the fact clear to participants that study of the Steps is not the same as working the Steps. Study is for understanding. More time is required to apply the Steps thoroughly to his or her life.

Groups can accomplish a short-term study of the Steps — an overview — in 13 weeks with one week for introduction and one week for each Step. Use the material from the group leadership models for learning activities in the study. If more than 13 weeks are available for your study, you may expand the study by adding any number of weeks to the longer Steps.

You may decide to do such a study as an open group or as the closed "discovery" group model. See for example the study guidelines for *Search for Significance* LIFE Support Edition or for *Untangling Relationships: A Christian Perspective on Codependency*.

Here is a recommended format for a short-term Step study.

1. Opening prayer (1 min.)
2. Read the Christ-Centered 12 Steps (3 min.)
3. Read the *Conquering Chemical Dependency* Principles, page 64 (optional)
4. Step study (45-60 min.)
5. Read the "Declaration," page 59 (1 min.)
6. Close with the Lord's Prayer or the Serenity Prayer (1 min.)

How to Lead a 12-Step Group

Avoid Controlling

Addiction is a condition marked by compulsive controlling. Group facilitators or leaders must beware of the urge to control the group. The facilitator or leader of a 12-Step group begins the group process and then allows the Holy Spirit to guide.

The facilitator occasionally may need to intervene in case of a problem, but if he or she feels a need to intervene often, the problem probably exists with the facilitator rather than with the group. In my experience with many years of group leadership, the most difficult thing to learn is to trust the Holy Spirit—allowing God to work through the process.

Starting the Meeting

So how does a facilitator start the meeting? First ask someone to read the preamble or welcome statement and the Steps. Either you or someone you choose may read the information. Make a clear statement about confidentiality. At each meeting explain simply but clearly, "What you hear at this meeting remains here."

Encourage people to understand that attendance at meetings is only part of the program. Explain that life change occurs by completing the Step work and working with a sponsor (provided your group has the capability of providing sponsors).

On pages 58-59 in the newcomer's pack you will find a suggested welcome and preamble statement. Be sure that newcomers receive preliminary information about the group and that they understand that they may share or pass during the sharing time.

You begin the sharing portion of the meeting. Explain the topic for the meeting and share a part of your own pilgrimage of recovery. In this section I have given you some sample topics for meetings. Later in this guide you will find sample leadership models for every Step and for every lesson in *Conquering Chemical Dependency*.

These are only representative of the hundreds of possible topics. Any of the key beliefs of the recovery process, any of the slogans, or any of the scriptural truths can form the basis for the sharing in a meeting.

Using Scripture in a Meeting

One word about Scripture is in order. The Word of God is our foundation. It is our authority and the basis of everything we hope and believe. For many people who are chemically dependent, the Scripture automatically signals failure and guilt. Enormous emotional content—much of it negative—is tied to the Scriptures. Damage, not healing, will result if the facilitator uses Scripture to control or condemn.

The following guidelines will help you avoid the pitfalls about use of Scripture in the group:

1. When you lead a meeting of any sort, use "I" messages and not "you" messages. When using Scripture, take extra care to avoid "you" messages. An "I" message involves saying something like, "This happened the other day. . . and I realized that this aspect of my addiction was at work." A subtle form of a "you" message might begin, "I read this in the Scripture, and it tells us how we may overcome. . . ." Remember that the Holy Spirit works through this process as we share *our* experience, strength, and hope—not as we tell others what their experience, strength, and hope should be.

2. When leading a meeting, but especially when using Scripture, emphasize how the passage speaks to your specific recovery. For example, I might share how reading Ecclesiastes 10:1 really spoke to me in a moment when I was tempted to rescue and control one of my children. Ecclesiastes 10:1 says, "Dead flies make a perfumer's oil stink, so a little foolishness is weightier than wisdom and honor." I read the verse and realized that a little foolishness can undo much progress. With my alcoholism, for me to drink one time would risk everything I have. "A little foolishness outweighs wisdom and honor," the Scripture says. In the same way, a little manipulation on my part can offset much of the progress I have made with my children.

3. Share horizontally rather than vertically. Share as a fellow struggler; don't teach down to people who have problems while you give the impression that you have none. The group process works on the principle of confession. When we hear others honestly share their struggles, sins, and successes, our own denial seems to fall away. We suddenly realize, "Hey, that's my story, too." Nothing kills the power of a meeting like a

facilitator who tells "these poor people how I solved my problems." Share your humanity . . . and leave your divinity at home!

We encourage all facilitators and group leaders to take the LIFE course *WiseCounsel*. In *WiseCounsel* John Drakeford teaches about "modeling the role." The more clearly you understand modeling the role, the better you can understand the goal for the group.

In an effective 12-Step group, group members model the role for each other. Even if you cannot take the course at this time, you will benefit from reading unit 3 of *WiseCounsel*.

Guiding the Sharing

How will your group deal with the mechanics of sharing? Here, as elsewhere in the 12-Step tradition, flexibility exists. In some meetings sharing occurs one at a time around the circle with little interaction permitted. In other meetings people follow no order for sharing. The leader shares the topic, and whoever desires to share does so.

Some of the most productive meetings involve a fluid topic—the leader shares the topic; then as people share, the topic may change. Learn to distinguish between healthy positive sharing and cross-talk. Cross-talk occurs when one member starts to speak to another member to "help." The discussion becomes a conversation—sometimes a debate—between two or more members of the group.

Healthy sharing respects the principle of responsibility. Allow the Holy Spirit to lead the person to the answer. Don't demean the person by giving answers that will confirm the suspicion that he or she cannot make good choices without depending on another person.

Prohibiting cross-talk does not mean discussion should not occur in a healthy group. With time and maturity both leader and group will learn to avoid cross-talk. In the early days of a group, structured sharing may avoid this hazard.

Sample Ways to Launch a Meeting

Here are some examples of ways to begin the sharing. After the opening prayer and reading of preliminary information the leader can share in this manner—
1. Our topic tonight is "Fear of Authority Figures." One of the characteristics of addiction with which I struggle

is fear of authority figures. I realize that I put people in the position of authority when doing so makes no sense. The other night I was in a restaurant. The server messed up the order and brought my son the wrong order. I am on a tight budget. What she brought cost more, and it wasn't what my son wanted, but I found myself saying to the server, "Oh, that's all right. I must not have spoken clearly enough." Then I realized what I was doing. My recovery kicked in. I realized I was setting an example for my children that would continue the sickness in our family. I called the server back. I politely but clearly said, "This was not what he ordered. Please bring us. . . ." Through that experience I realized that I had been making the server an authority figure for me.

2. The topic for today's meeting is based on the slogan, "If nothing changes, nothing changes." Recently I realized that I am really good at working my program in my head. But I want to stop the cycle of dysfunctional behavior in my family. I realized that my children don't see what goes on in my head; they only see what I say and do. So I did an inventory. I looked at the key parts of my addiction. I made a list of my unhealthy behaviors. That list includes being a people pleaser, being a martyr, being passive, and being a perfectionist. During the time I was working the Steps with my sponsor, I discovered that these were my particular habits on which I have to keep working the Steps. So I wrote my personal habits on a card, and I ask myself once a day, "How did I do today on people pleasing? and so forth." As we share today, from where you are in recovery, how are you doing with identifying and/or changing unhealthy habits? Because if nothing changes, nothing changes.

3. The topic for tonight is "Recovery is a messy business." I have been a rescuer for a long time. I realize that I am unrealistic to expect the people I've caretaken suddenly to begin to be responsible for themselves. So I'm having to establish some boundaries in my life and risk other people getting angry or unhappy because I'm not doing what they want. (Share a personal example.) Here is a Scripture that teaches that progress comes with problems. Proverbs 14:4 says, "Where no oxen are, the manger is clean, But much increase comes by the strength of the ox." Oxen are messy animals. A farmer in the Middle East in Bible times wouldn't keep the stall vacant simply because an ox might make a mess. That Scripture reminds me that some messes, or challenging situations, can accompany recovery. I cannot expect my family members to say, "Wow! I'm so glad you are in recovery. Now I won't expect you to take care of my responsibilities for me any longer. I instantly will adapt by changing my

behavior." I am learning to expect some challenges, but I know that the end results are worth the effort.

4. I have been doing some personal work related to Step 2. Before I entered recovery, I didn't realize how my parents shaped my view of, and especially my feelings about, God. After doing a great deal of work, I realize how I really have felt about God. I felt He criticized everything I did and that I never could please Him. And I felt He had abandoned or would abandon me. I am discovering that my feelings about God don't represent who He really is at all. I am getting acquainted with the God who is real and whom I can trust. As we share, the topic is our concept of God. How close is what you feel about God to who you believe God really is?

5. Tonight the topic is forgiveness. Recently I heard somebody say, "All you people in recovery are just blaming your parents." I thought about that, and it really bothered me. Here is what I've concluded. My parents were just like me. They loved their children just like I love mine. I think almost all parents do. Identifying how my family, for generations, has taught dysfunctional messages is not disloyalty to my parents. I can forgive them and forgive myself by realizing how the process works. What stops real forgiveness is denial. Until I break through the denial and honestly admit what happened, I can't forgive myself or my parents.

These examples are only models for a 12-Step sharing meeting. The concept is simple.

• State the topic for the meeting.
• Share yourself.
• Share a personal example from your life.
• Share from an attitude of humility.

Share your hope of success, but always share out of your humanity. Remember when you were a child, you hated to hear adults tell you how they walked 12 miles to school, uphill, both ways? The reason you hated it was because they were sharing down at you.

Above all, pray and follow the Holy Spirit's leading. At many of the best meetings I ever attended, one of two things happened. Either the leader simply said, "No topic; tonight, just share where you are in your recovery," or the people in the group disregarded the topic and shared where they were anyway.

Facilitating a group requires more humility and restraint than it does anything else. In our answers-oriented faith, being quiet is difficult. Humility is required when you know the answer but you also know the person ideally discovers the answer for himself or herself.

How to Be a Sponsor

The apprenticeship or disciple-making relationship with a sponsor is vital to the 12-Step process. By serving as sponsor you will experience some of the greatest personal and spiritual growth in your life. A basic set of principles to help you do the work of a sponsor follow.

1. **Have a sponsor and be working the Steps actively.** Don't attempt to lead others where you have not been or at least are going. Ideally sponsors have one to two years or more in recovery.

The problem with the availability of sponsors is obvious. In the beginning of a 12-Step ministry, where do you find these sponsors? If you are starting a new program, you may find Christian sponsors from other 12-Step groups. In your church you may find individuals who have recovery experience. If no such sponsors exist, you may form a "buddy-system" partnership with another member of the group. You may have to sponsor each other. Although this approach is not the ideal one, every group has to start somewhere, and it does work. Even when your groups develop some maturity, you probably will continue to have a shortage of sponsors so that you continue to need to use a "buddy system."

2. **Establish and maintain clear boundaries and lines of responsibility and accountability.** Make clear how you will hold the person accountable. Avoid enabling or controlling relationships. The goal of being a sponsor is not to rescue or repair. The person you sponsor is the worker. The goal is to allow individuals to "work the Steps" for themselves. You may see yourself as an encourager, a listener, and a catalyst for those doing the work. Beware of feeling that you are responsible for his or her performance.

Sometimes a sponsor supplies encouragement, sometimes an objective point of view. Often people in recovery become "stuck" in a particular situation or on a particular Step. You can help the person you sponsor to brainstorm options and find ways to move forward. Remember that an effective sponsor seldom gives answers and does not take the responsibility that belongs to another.

3. **Be a listener** . Listening is one of the most difficult skills to develop. Often people's greatest need is for someone to listen to them with attentiveness. By listening you are giving a priceless gift to a person whom others have treated with disrespect. By not providing answers you are affirming your confidence in the person. You are saying, "I believe you are capable of making wise decisions. You do not have to depend on someone else to tell you what to do." For assistance in developing listening skills see unit 4 of *WiseCounsel: Skills for Lay Counseling*.

4. **Encourage the grieving process.** Many of the problems of addiction and codependency involve incomplete grieving. When we have "stuffed" or buried painful emotions and hurtful experiences from the past, we must surface our losses and grieve them. Usually we are reluctant, if not resistant, to feel these painful feelings. A sponsor can challenge us to face our fear of emotion.

My sponsor's favorite line is, "You're in your head again." My natural response to the approach of emotional pain is to intellectualize. My sponsor has aided me greatly by challenging me to get "out of my head" and to feel my emotions.

In the final portion of this chapter I have suggested some useful ways to assist persons you sponsor to deal with their incomplete grief. One person I sponsored said to me, "You just want to see me cry, don't you?" I responded by sharing my experience with grieving—that until I grieve my losses, I cannot get beyond them. Then I asked, "What losses do you have that you have not grieved?" Later my friend thanked me for encouraging him to do the difficult work of grieving.

5. **Model responsibility.** At the first meeting, explain clearly the boundaries of the relationship. Explain that because you are a recovering person, you cannot rescue or fix the other person. Clearly state the amount of time you can spend with the person, where you can meet, how often you can meet, and the nature of the sponsoring relationship. Share what you expect of the person you sponsor. For example, I explain that I will assign work to be done (such as, "Complete the written work in Step 1 of *Conquering Chemical Dependency*."), then the person calls me when he or she completes the work and is ready to meet. I say, "I am available. I encourage you to call me when you are upset, struggling, tempted to drink or use, or just stuck, but I will not do your work for you or try to make you do your work. You are responsible for your recovery." I

then may call the person I am sponsoring, but I will call only to convey friendship and interest. The person must make the appointment to review Step work. No norm exists for how often the sponsor and sponsoree meet; the frequency depends on the motivation of the sponsoree and how quickly he or she processes the Steps.

Model responsibility in another way. Set realistic boundaries on the number of people you sponsor. A general guideline would be to sponsor at one time no more than two people who are actively working the Steps. A better guideline may be to sponsor only one person who is actively working the Steps. After a person has done the initial Step work, you will continue to be his or her sponsor, but the relationship changes to that of colleague. You then may have time to begin sponsoring another person who is actively working the Steps.

You easily can allow the needs of others and the feeling of being needed to lead you to overcommitment and back to addictive behavior. I knew I was in trouble on this matter when I sat in a meeting with several people who shared about their relationship with their sponsor—and all of them were talking about me! You will struggle with this issue. Try to err on the side of caution.

What Does a Sponsor Actually Do?

An effective sponsor follows the guidelines above, but specifically what is the sponsor to do? The sponsor is filling the role parents ideally would have played in a person's life. Here are some helps for sponsors:

1. In the beginning, help the person understand the three parts of the program—group for emotional support, Step work done by the person, and relationship with the sponsor for listening and encouragement necessary to work the Steps.

2. Listen as the person reviews each Step in *Conquering Chemical Dependency*. You may ask the person to read his or her answers to you. You may choose another way to allow the person to review the Step work.

3. Give special attention to the written prayers the member's book asks the member to write. Some people have no particular difficulty communicating with God. For others prayer is a great problem. Writing prayers can be a powerful experience in some individuals' lives.

4. Encourage the process of grief and catharsis. Catharsis involves relieving hidden fears and emotional issues by bringing them to the surface and expressing them. You may see the need for the person to express anger and grief through letters to God, parents, or other significant people in the person's past. Make those assignments as necessary and listen as the person reads the letters he or she has written. Note that such assignments are to deal with emotions, not to cause harm by being mailed to living individuals.

5. As part of Step 4, assign the person to write a history of his or her chemical dependency.

6. Every sponsor must determine how involved and demanding he or she will be. You may find yourself facing difficult decisions. What will you do if a person you sponsor is committing illegal actions like driving under the influence? What will you do if the possibility of suicide or violence exists? My personal approach is to attempt to be as honest as possible from the beginning. I tell the person that if necessary for his own good I will get him arrested or committed. You need to determine how "hard-nosed" you are willing to be.

The Changing Nature of Sponsorship

As a person works the Steps, the sponsor relationship changes. In the beginning the sponsor is the authority. In time, the relationship changes to that of colleague. As you listen and encourage, be aware of this changing relationship. Don't allow your feelings and your need to be needed to stand in the way of this healthy change. The goal of parenting is to produce independent people who no longer need the parent. In the same way the goal of sponsoring is to work one's self out of a job.

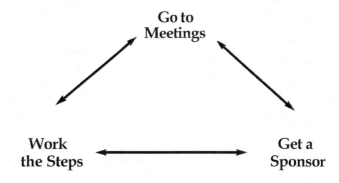

Special Issues Related to Chemical Dependency

Several specialized issues are particularly important for leaders of a chemical dependency support group ministry.

1. Which Book to Use? Because of differences in life situations, length of sobriety, and reading ability, we have produced two member's books. *Conquering Chemical Dependency: A Christ-Centered 12-Step Process* is the primary member's workbook. *Conquering Chemical Dependency: First Steps to a Christ-Centered 12-Step Process*—sometimes simply referred to as *First Steps*—is the 64-page version.

We have designed *First Steps* for people who are new to recovery and who are not ready for the full-length member's book. *First Steps* also is the best choice for people with limited reading ability or who have difficulty concentrating because of such factors as the effects of drugs or learning disabilities. No chapter in *First Steps* is more than six pages in length.

People who have more time in sobriety will benefit more from the full-length workbook. The ideal situation might be for the newcomer to work through *First Steps* and then work through the Steps in more detail by using the longer workbook. Note that both books contain distinctive content so that the person who uses both will not simply be repeating his or her previous work.

2. Combined or Separate Groups? You easily may combine into a single group people who are working through the 224-page workbook and people who are working through *First Steps*. If your groups are following a traditional 12-Step format, the issues and sharing time will be the primary focus of the meetings.

The member who is working the Steps with a sponsor will be the primary user of the workbook. In the group leadership models for each Step we have given some distinctive helps for a group using primarily or exclusively *First Steps*, but remember that a leader of a *First Steps* group may share in the group a concept or topic from the 224-page version.

3. Be Alert for Related Issues: Many people who have addictive disorders grew up in dysfunctional family situations. These recovering individuals may identify the fact that they need additional recovery from codependency or other issues.

People sometimes ask at what point in recovery a person can begin safely to deal with related issues. Recovery from a chemical addiction might be called stage one recovery. Chemical addiction may be termed a primary addiction—immediately life-threatening.

The first critical need for a person recovering from chemical dependency is to establish sobriety or abstinence. While codependency or sexual-abuse issues may underlie and support a primary addiction, and while the abuse issues need to be addressed and resolved, a major danger exists when a person attempts to accomplish too much too fast.

As persons grow in sobriety, they then will be able to turn their attention to the underlying issues in recovery. People need to become stable and free from chemicals and then begin to address patterns and concerns such as control, unexpressed grief, and unresolved hurt. These issues affect every other relationship in a recovering person's life.

While doing the work of recovery, a person may discover particular issues of which he or she was not previously aware. The person may not be aware that certain behaviors are destructive.

Resolving the problems which arise out of abuse sometimes is a key to lasting recovery. Some of the issues dealt with in recovery from chemical dependency are the same concerns involved in codependency or sexual abuse, but other issues are different.

Part of recovery from codependency or sexual abuse includes remembering and dealing with pain from the past. Persons who are not solidly established in their recovery easily can dredge up more pain than they can stand. The stress can lead them to relapse. For this reason, be alert for related issues, but keep the focus of the group on recovery from chemical dependency.

4. The Need for Referral: Because of the health risks and the concerns that related issues pose, give attention to the matter of referral. Maintain a relationship with a medical doctor who has experience in the area of chemical dependency. In the same way, maintain a relationship with a professional Christian counselor to advise you when critical needs arise. See page 13 in this facilitator's guide and unit 2 of *WiseCounsel* for help in developing a referral list.

Admitting My Powerlessness

Step 1

We admit that by ourselves we are powerless over chemical substances—that our lives have become unmanageable.

◇ Goals for Step 1

1. Learn about the addiction process and begin to evaluate the effects of addiction in your life.
2. Identify the progress of chemical dependency in your life.
3. Describe your chemical use.
4. Examine your life for signs of unmanageability.
5. Describe a process for confronting denial and for accepting reality.

Before the Meeting

❑ Read and complete the learning activities for Step 1 in the *Conquering Chemical Dependency* member's book.

❑ Find a quiet time and place to pray for group members by name. Ask the Lord to give you the wisdom you need to prepare for and to lead the group meeting.

❑ Read the Group Leadership Models section which follows. The section provides activities that relate to each lesson in Step 1. Select the activities that best suit your group members' needs. Be aware that this section provides far more activities than you will have time to use during your meeting. If you are using the 13-week overview schedule, in which you spend only one week on each Step, you likely will use a few activities from this Step. If you use the Step Study schedule, you may use several of the activities before your group moves on to another Step. If you are following the traditional 12-Step format, the leader will select for the meeting one topic from one of the examples given or from the leader's experience.

❑ Arrange the chairs. Many chemically dependent people may feel trapped in a circle arrangement of chairs. If you use a circle, leave an opening in the circle so such members won't feel trapped.

❑ If you select an activity that involves a handout, make enough copies of the handout for each group member to have one.

Group Leadership Models:

Lesson 1: Where Did It Begin?

Make and distribute copies of handout number 1 (page 52 of this facilitator's guide.) Explain the activity and give group members time to circle the words in the paragraph. Tell a portion of your story by relating your responses to the activity. Invite members to share how they feel about the activity.

Make and distribute copies of handout number 2 (page 52.) Briefly explain the checklist. Explain that members will not have to show their answers to the group. Allow group members to fill out the checklist. Share your response to the checklist (not necessarily your answers but how you feel about the activity). Invite sharing.

Make and distribute copies of handout number 3 (page 53). Explain the chart on the handout. Explain that a place on the chart exists for everyone who ever has taken a drink or used a mood-altering substance. Explain that because the activity is private, members will not be asked to share their responses. Ask group members to mark the spot that best represents the progress of their experience with chemicals. Share part of your story and how you react to the chart. Invite group members to share what the chart tells them about themselves and their relationship to chemicals.

Relate the story of the businessman on page 12 of the member's book. Briefly explain the progressive nature of addiction. Share your reaction to the awareness of your addiction. Share your statement from the learning activity following the story of the businessman. Encourage members to share their reaction and their feelings about the concept.

Lesson 2: The Stages of Addiction

Read the first four paragraphs of the lesson from the member's book and summarize it for group members.

Relate the slogan, "I don't have a drinking problem, I have a living problem." Explain that the 12 Steps help us make progress toward the goal of an effective, Christ-honoring l ife. Share your reaction to the concepts in the passage. Invite members to share how they feel about realizing our "living problem."

Relate Craig Naaken's definition of addiction as "a pathological love and trust relationship with some object or event"[1]. Explain that we develop a relationship with our addiction that begins like a romance and leads to an illicit affair. Tell how your addiction resembles a romance. Possibly include the grief you experienced when you realized that your drug of choice was not good for you. Invite sharing.

Make and distribute copies of handout number 4, the stages of addiction (page 53 of the facilitator's guide.) Allow members time to check their responses. Share something about your story as it relates to the stages of addiction. Be careful not to glorify your experiences while using and not to create a climate of competition for members to see which of them has the most horrible story. As you share, keep the emphasis on your realization of powerlessness and on recovery. Invite sharing.

Lesson 3: Powerlessness

Explain that the paradox of addiction is that the more we struggle in our own power against the object of our addiction, the greater is the addiction's hold over our lives. Share the key concept from lesson 3: "Drug use makes me feel powerful and in control while it makes me powerless." Share something about your own struggle to accept the reality of your powerlessness. Encourage members to share their struggles.

Explain that powerlessness is the distinguishing mark of all addiction. Summarize the three paragraphs that begin lesson 3. Share how denial made it difficult for you to admit your addiction. Invite members to share how denial has affected their lives.

Read on page 19 of the member's book about the concept of euphoric recall. Share this concept with group members. Share how euphoric recall kept you going back to your drug of choice even while it was making your life more unmanageable. Ask members to share their experiences in this area.

Pass sheets of blank paper to group members. Read on page 20 of the member's book about the concept of the

time line. Explain this concept to group members. Allow members time to draw their own time line of their drug use. Share how your time line helps you objectively see your powerlessness and unmanageability. Encourage members to share how the time line helps them to see their situations.

Lesson 4: Unmanageable

Read on pages 22-23 of the member's book the stories of Susan, Ray, Judy, and Richard. Lead a brief discussion of each story in which the group members identify the area of unmanageability in each story. Explain that unmanageability does not mean that our lives are totally out of control. Unmanageability means that our drug use makes one or more areas out of control with the result that our lives cannot be directed. Share something about how your drug use made your life unmanageable. Encourage members to share.

Explain that one of the ways addiction makes our lives unmanageable relates to values. Our drug use and the resultant protecting our supply, hiding our behaviors, and seeking to avoid responsibility inevitably leads us to compromise our value systems. We do and say things we thought we never would do or say. Share several ways your drug use led you to violate your value system (see the learning activity on page 24 of the member's book). Encourage members to share ways their using led them to set their value systems aside.

Make and distribute copies of handout number 5 (page 54). Explain that answers will be confidential. Allow time for members to fill out the checklist. Share your reaction about the checklist. Ask members to share what they learned about themselves by completing the checklist.

Lesson 5: Reality

Explain the concept that begins the lesson in the member's book—that taking the first Step is not a surrender of our power but is a decision to live in reality. Share your own journey about taking the Step. Ask members to share their journeys.

Briefly explain the perplexing yet important fact that when we begin recovery, we enter a grief process. When we give up our drug of choice, we feel as though our closest friend died or rejected us. Share something about your journey through the grief process in

28

recovery. Ask members to tell about their own experiences in this area.

After you review page 27 of the member's book, briefly explain the stages of the grieving process. Relate that we do not progress through the stages in a straight-line fashion but rather cycle through them in a variety of ways. From your experience share some examples of the stages. Encourage members to share how they relate to the various stages of grief.

❖ *First Steps* : Admitting My Powerlessness

(Remember that you may use the group leadership models or handouts as appropriate from the full-size member's book even if you are leading a *First Steps* group.)

Make and distribute copies of handout number 2, page 52 of the facilitator's guide. Briefly explain the checklist. Explain that members will not be asked to show their answers to the group. Allow group members to fill out the checklist. Share your response about the checklist (not necessarily your answers but how you respond to the activity). Ask members to share their responses.

Pass sheets of blank paper to group members. Explain the concept of the time line that appears on page 9 of *First Steps*. Allow members time to draw their own time line of their drug use. Share how your time line helps you objectively see your powerlessness and unmanageability. Invite members to share how the time line helps them to see their situations.

Make and distribute copies of handout number 5 (page 54). Explain that answers will be confidential. Allow time for members to fill out the checklist. Share your reaction about the checklist. Invite members to share what they learned about themselves by completing the checklist.

On page 64 of the facilitator's guide we have printed the course map that appears at the end of *Conquering Chemical Dependency: A Christ-Centered 12-Step Process*. Some facilitators may not have access to this 224-page book and may find the course map useful as a learning aid to help them and their group members visualize the 12-Step process.

After the Meeting

❏ Read "Before the Meeting" for Step 2 on page 30 of the facilitator's guide to evaluate the amount of preparation you will need for your next meeting. Record at the top of page 30 a time when you will prepare.
❏ Study carefully Step 2 and complete all the exercises in the *Conquering Chemical Dependency* member's book.

[1]Craig Naaken, *The Addictive Personality: Understanding the Compulsion in Our Lives*, (Center City, MN: Hazelden Foundation, 1988).

Coming to Believe

Step 2

We come to believe that God, through Jesus Christ, can restore us to sanity.

◇ **Goals for Step 2**

1. Identify attitudes and actions characteristic of distorted thinking.
2. Describe the effects on your life of guilt and blame.
3. Analyze past relationships with your parents.
4. Describe the impact of your past relationships on your view of God.
5. Act to correct elements of your faulty concept of God.
6. Act to correct elements of your faulty self-concept.

Before the Meeting

❏ Read and complete the learning activities for Step 2 in the *Conquering Chemical Dependency* member's book.
❏ Find a quiet time and place to pray for group members by name. Ask the Lord to give you the wisdom you need to prepare for and to lead the group meeting.
❏ Read the Group Leadership Models section which follows. The section provides activities that relate to each lesson in Step 2. Select the activities that best suit your group members' needs. Be aware that this section provides far more activities than you will have time to use during your meeting.
❏ Arrange the chairs.
❏ If you select an activity that involves a handout, make enough copies of the handout for each group member to have one.

Group Leadership Models

Lesson 1: Restore Us to Sanity

Make and distribute copies of handout 6 (page 54). Explain that insanity does not refer to a mental disease. It means exercising unsound judgment. Share your reaction to the examples of insanity by sharing how you have used some of the examples in your life. Invite group members to share their reactions about the checklist.

After you read the application of Proverbs 14:1 from page 34 of the member's book, briefly explain it to group members. Share your answer to the learning activity from page 34 of the member's book—five occasions when you have acted in such a way that an objective observer might say, "That's insane." Invite group members to share how their addictions have led them to insane behavior.

Lesson 2: The Origin of Our Concept of God

Briefly explain the information from the first two paragraphs of the lesson about God's plan for our development. Tell group members that sin damaged God's plan so that we all develop a distorted view of God. Share your answer to the learning activity about how your family experiences and choices have affected your relationship with God. Ask group members to share about this topic.

After reading page 36 of the member's book about the operation of guilt, briefly explain it to the group. Share how guilt has affected your self-esteem and your relationships with your family, with others, and with God. Invite sharing.

Read pages 36-37 of the member's book and summarize for group members the paragraphs about blame. Share how you feel when you fail, what you call yourself, and how you respond to others when they fail. Encourage members to share how blame affects their lives.

After reading the learning activity and margin box on page 37, explain to group members about the ways we condemn others. Share something about the methods you use to blame. Share how you feel when you use blame and how you are changing your behavior. Invite group members to share about these two topics.

Lesson 3: Your Parents and You

Explain that a part of recovery includes studying our families of origin. By comparing our feelings about and relationships with our parents, we can learn much about ourselves. Explain that we do not study family of origin so that we can blame or so that we can simply feel the emotions. We do not study to stay stuck in the past. We study our family of origin to understand how we have become what we are so that we can move forward into the future. Share something you have learned about yourself through the study of your family of origin. Encourage others to share what they've learned.

Relate that many of us need to express our feelings toward our parents and that writing letters is a valuable means of doing so. Share your experience with the letters this lesson calls for. Invite members to share their own experiences with the assignments if they have completed them or to share their feelings about the process if they have not.

Lesson 4: Your Relationship with God

Briefly explain that we derive our image of God largely from our parents or caretakers. An important recovery task is to compare our concept of God with the reality of God as He reveals Himself to us in Scripture. Share what you learned about your concept of God through working this lesson. Invite group members to tell what they learned.

Lesson 5: Believing the Truth About God

Explain that every person's greatest task in life is to know God as He really is. Relate that we have a concept of God in our intellect and emotions, but that is not who God really is. Share how studying Psalm 139 has impacted your life and how you are knowing God through His Word. Invite group members to share either where they are in their journey to get to know God or how the Psalm has impacted their view of God. Be sure to allow members to "be where they really are" in this regard; do not allow any person to tell what other members "should" feel.

Lesson 6: Believing the Truth About You

Make copies of handout 7—the false beliefs, painful emotions, and God's truths. Briefly explain the chart. Share how the truths of God are changing your thinking and your life. Invite members to share their reactions about the chart. Remind members that God desires honesty more than He does "good" answers. Make certain that members are safe in sharing whatever they feel with freedom to know that other group members will not "correct" or "fix" them.

❖ *First Steps* : Coming to Believe

Remember that even if your group is using *Conquering Chemical Dependency: First Steps to a Christ-Centered 12-Step Process,* you still can use handouts or group leadership models from the full-size member's book.

Make and distribute copies of handout 6—the 11 examples of insanity. Explain that insanity does not refer to a mental disease. It means exercising unsound judgment. Share your reaction to the examples of insanity by sharing how you have used some of the examples in your life. Invite group members to share their reactions to the checklist.

Explain that a part of recovery includes studying our families of origin. By comparing our feelings about and relationships with our parents, we can learn much about ourselves. Explain that we do not study family of origin to blame or simply to feel the emotions. We do not study to stay stuck in the past. We study our family of origin to understand how we have become what we are so that we can move forward into the future. Share something about what you have learned about yourself through studying your family of origin. Invite sharing.

After the Meeting

❏ Read "Before the Meeting" for Step 3 on page 32 of the facilitator's guide to evaluate the amount of preparation you will need for your next group meeting. Record at the top of page 32 a time when you will prepare.
❏ Study carefully Step 3 and complete all the exercises in the *Conquering Chemical Dependency* member's book.

Turning It Over

Step 3

We make a decision to turn our will and our lives over to God through Jesus Christ.

◇ **Goals for Unit 3**

1. Describe the twofold nature of Step 3.
2. Describe the biblical concept of repentance.
3. Describe the complete forgiveness Christ gives.
4. Have an opportunity to express personal faith in God.
5. Describe the ongoing process of applying Step 3 to practical problems.

Before the Meeting

❏ Read and complete the learning activities for Step 3 in the *Conquering Chemical Dependency* member's book.

❏ Find a quiet time and place to pray for group members by name. Ask the Lord to give you the wisdom you need to prepare for and to lead the group meeting.

❏ Read the Group Leadership Models section which follows. The section provides activities that relate to each lesson in Step 3. Select the activities that best suit your group members' needs. Be aware that this section provides far more activities than you will have time to use during your meeting. Just as a reminder about which activities to choose, you likely will use only a few activities from this Step if you are using the 13-week overview schedule. If you use the Step Study schedule, you may use a number of the activities before your group moves on to another Step. If you are following the traditional 12-Step format, the leader will select for the meeting one topic from one of the examples given or from the leader's experience.

❏ Arrange the chairs.

❏ If you select an activity that involves a handout, make enough copies of the handout for each group member to have one.

Group Leadership Models:

Lesson 1: Why Step 3?

Read Richard's story on pages 55 and 56 in the member's book. Relate the story to group members. Read Romans 6:16. Share something about your story regarding the truth of the passage—see the learning activity on page 56. Invite group members to share the similarity between their story and Richard's story.

Explain the twofold nature of Step 3 (page 57 of the member's book). Share a brief testimony about when and how you received Jesus as Savior. Share how you first took the Step as it pertains to your addiction. Encourage members to tell where they currently see themselves in relation to the third Step.

Lesson 2: A Change of Mind

Read the opening paragraph of Lesson 2 about self-will. State that all our addictions are painful results of our out-of-control self-will. Share your responses to the learning activity (pages 58-59). Explain how your self-will has damaged the four areas of your life. Share something about how working the program is changing these areas of your life. Invite group members to discuss how self-will has harmed them and how the recovery process is repairing that damage.

Read on page 59 the story from the book *Alcoholics Anonymous*. Relate the story to group members. Explain that what the psychiatrist described was a restructuring of the man's mind and personality. That transformation is what the Bible calls repentance. Explain that repentance does not merely represent the way we become Christians. Repentance is the ongoing process of God transforming our lives. Share a recent experience in which God changed your mind in a practical way. Ask other group members to share their experiences.

Lesson 3: Your Position in Christ

Relate the stories, from page 61 of the member's book, of David, who thought that he must clean up his life before God would accept him, and of Lisa, who thought her sins were too great for God to forgive. Share how you have come to accept God's grace as full payment for your sins. Invite sharing.

Explain the concept of propitiation (page 62 of the member's book). Do not attempt to explain the concept entirely—propitiation involves the entire Old Testament sacrificial system. The key is that Jesus completely has taken the blame for our sin. He has left no blame for us. Share how your feelings about blame have changed since you have begun to understand and accept God's gift of propitiation. Encourage members to share their feelings about God's complete forgiveness.

Lesson 4: Working the Step, Part One

Remind group members that Step 3 applies in two ways. Share the fact that for this meeting the emphasis will be on applying the Step to our eternal relationship with God. Summarize the section of the member's book (page 65) about trusting in Christ. Share your personal testimony about how you have come to trust in Christ. Invite members to share their progress in relation to the eternal application of the Step. Emphasize that members work on this Step progressively—people continually work on their relationship with God. Also emphasize the next to last paragraph of the lesson (page 66) about instant deliverance.

Lesson 5: Working the Step, Part Two

Read Colossians 2:6. Explain that the verse says we are to continue to live the life God has given us in the same way that we received Christ. Share one or more examples of how you have applied the Step to practical problems in your life. Explain that this principle is not about being perfect but is about turning issues over to God as they arise. You may desire to share instances of failure also. Remind the group members that our hope is not in our ability to hold on but is in God's promise of faithfulness. Encourage group members to share how they have applied this principle to their lives.

❖ *First Steps* : Turning It Over

Read Donna's story on page 17 in *First Steps*. Relate the story to group members. Read Romans 6:16. Share something about your story regarding the truth of the passage—see the learning activity on page 17. Invite group members to share the similarity between their stories and Donna's story.

Explain that Step 3 includes both a decision to turn over to God our eternal destiny and to turn over our daily struggles. Share a brief testimony about when and how you received Jesus as Savior. Share how you first took the Step as it pertains to your addiction. Encourage members to tell where they currently see themselves in relation to the third Step.

Read the article (page 20 of *First Steps*) entitled "An Unpleasant Surprise." Share something about your experience with the grief process in recovery. Invite members to share about their experiences with grief in recovery.

After the Meeting

❏ Read "Before the Meeting" for Step 4 on page 34 of the facilitator's guide to evaluate the amount of preparation you will need for your next group meeting. Record at the top of page 34 a time when you will prepare.
❏ Study carefully Step 4 and complete all the exercises in the *Conquering Chemical Dependency* member's book.

Taking My Inventory

Step 4

We make a searching, courageous moral inventory of ourselves.

◇ Goals for Step 4

1. Describe a moral inventory.
2. Write an inventory of dishonesty and resentment.
3. Write an inventory of self-pity and false pride.
4. Write an inventory of criticism and destructive anger.
5. Write an inventory of fear and impatience.

Before the Meeting

❑ Read and complete the learning activities for Step 4 in the *Conquering Chemical Dependency* member's book.

❑ Find a quiet time and place to pray for group members by name. Ask the Lord to give you the wisdom you need to prepare for and to lead the group meeting.

❑ Read the Group Leadership Models section which follows. The section provides activities that relate to each lesson in Step 4. Select the activities that best suit your group members' needs. Be aware that this section provides far more activities than you will have time to use during your meeting. Just as a reminder about which activities to choose, you likely will use only a few activities from this Step if you are using the 13-week overview schedule. If you use the Step Study schedule, you may use several of the activities before your group moves on to another Step. If you are following the traditional 12-Step format, the leader will select for the meeting one topic from one of the examples given or from the leader's experience.

❑ Arrange the chairs.

❑ If you select an activity that involves a handout, make enough copies of the handout for each group member to have one.

Group Leadership Models

Lesson 1: Why Take a Moral Inventory?

Explain that an inventory is a "taking-stock" activity. When we conduct an inventory, we honestly list all the things, both good and bad, in our possession. Stress the importance of writing an inventory. By writing an inventory we become aware of many things we previously did not see. Explain that Step 4 is not an "immoral" inventory. (See explanation on page 72 of the member's book.) Share something about your growth through taking the Step. Encourage members to share about their own growth.

Summarize the member's book section beginning with "Trying to hide your flaws"(page 73). Explain that only by rigorous honesty can we break the cycle of guilt and denial that drives our addiction. Read the paragraph on page 73 which begins with "We can break the cycle." Share how taking your inventory has been important in your recovery. Ask others to tell their experiences.

Lesson 2: Dishonesty and Resentment

Relate one or more of the forms of dishonesty from the inventory (page 76-79). Share about how you are learning to face the dishonesty in your life. Tell about positive change that has occurred in your life as a result. Invite members to share progress in their journey to face and deal with dishonesty.

Define and explain resentment (page 78). Share how resentment has been a part of your life and how God is changing your life. Stress the benefits that come from the difficult task of facing and eliminating resentments. Ask members to share where they are in their journey to be rid of resentment.

Summarize and explain the member's book section about forgiveness (page 79). Explain that many people do not want to forgive because they have distorted ideas about forgiveness. State that forgiveness is a gift we give ourselves because it frees us to live effectively. Share something about your journey in learning to forgive. Ask others to tell about their own journeys in this area of forgiveness.

Lesson 3: Self-pity and False Pride

Make and distribute copies of Handout 8 (page 55)—Self-pity Characteristics. Summarize the member's book section entitled "Self-pity: How to be a Life-long Victim." Share your reaction to the characteristics in the handout and share which characteristics you checked. Invite members to share their reactions to one or more of the characteristics or to share how they are overcoming the self-pity trap.

Read the two paragraphs entitled "Gratitude: Cure for the 'Pity Party' Blues" (page 83). Share your responses to the two learning activities that follow. Share how you are learning to replace self-pity with gratitude. Encourage members to share their progress in learning to replace self-pity with gratitude.

Summarize the member's book section entitled "False Pride/False Humility: Two Sides of a Counterfeit Coin," page 83. Explain that in recovery we learn to replace our extreme thinking with a realistic evaluation of ourselves. Share one or more examples in which you have identified and are replacing your false pride or false humility. Invite others to share examples.

Explain that humility requires self-acceptance. Summarize "Humility: Having the Mind of Christ," page 84 of the member's book. Explain the parable of the chief seats at the feast. Share how you believe you would feel if you were so self-accepting that you could take joyfully the lowest seat at the banquet. Encourage members to tell how they are growing in self-acceptance or what they need to do to grow in self-acceptance.

Lesson 4: Criticism and Destructive Anger

Summarize the member's book section entitled "Criticism: Verbal Dissection" (page 87). Share the part criticism has played in your addiction and recovery. You may share how the criticism you have received has affected your life, but seek to share also how you have been guilty of criticizing others. Invite members to discuss the reasons for practicing criticism and what they are doing to overcome the habit of criticizing.

Summarize the member's book section on destructive anger (page 89). Emphasize the fact that we often are unable to forgive until we have acknowledged the full extent of the offense, expressed our anger, and purposed to forgive. Share something about your journey to replace anger with forgiveness. Invite sharing on this topic.

Lesson 5: Fear and Impatience

Read the member's book section entitled "Fear: God's Warning System" (page 91). Share something about your struggle with fear and how working the Steps helps to resolve the problem. Ask members to tell their experiences in dealing with fear.

❖ First Steps: My Moral Inventory

Explain that an inventory is a "taking-stock" activity. When we conduct an inventory of our homes or businesses, we honestly list all the things, both good and bad, in our possession. Stress the importance of writing an inventory. By writing an inventory we become aware of many things we previously did not see. Explain that Step 4 is not an "immoral" inventory but an honest assessment of our good and bad traits. Share something about how you grew as you took the Step. Encourage members to share about their own growth.

Describe the two areas of the personal inventory—self-defeating behaviors and improvements in one's character. Share at least one example of each area you identified by taking inventory. Share an area in which you have identified self-defeating behaviors such as control or self-centeredness, and share an area in which you have seen growth and improvement in your life. Invite group members to share one positive and one negative area in their lives.

After the Meeting

❑ Read "Before the Meeting" for Step 5 on page 36 of the facilitator's guide to evaluate the amount of preparation you will need for your next group meeting. Record at the top of page 36 a time when you will prepare.

❑ Study carefully Step 5 and complete all the exercises in the *Conquering Chemical Dependency* member's book.

Freedom Through Confession

Step 5
We admit to God, to ourselves, and to another person the exact nature of our wrongs.

◇ Goals for Step 5

1. Define *confession* and describe four benefits that come from confession.
2. Describe key biblical teachings about confession.
3. Make final preparation to share Step 5 with another person.

Before the Meeting

❏ Read and complete the learning activities for Step 5 in the *Conquering Chemical Dependency* member's book.

❏ Find a quiet time and place to pray for group members by name. Ask the Lord to give you the wisdom you need to prepare for and to lead the group meeting.

❏ Read the Group Leadership Models section which follows. The section provides activities that relate to each lesson in Step 5. Select the activities that best suit your group members' needs. Be aware that this section provides far more activities than you will have time to use during your meeting. Just as a reminder about which activities to choose, you likely will use only a few activities from this Step if you are using the 13-week overview schedule. If you use the Step Study schedule, you may use several of the activities before your group moves on to another Step. If you are following the traditional 12-Step format, the leader will select one topic from one of the examples given or from the leader's experience.

❏ Arrange the chairs.

❏ If you select an activity that involves a handout, make enough copies of the handout for each group member to have one.

Ask God to guide you as you seek a balance between providing activities while you allow enough time for spontaneous sharing. When you are in doubt about which direction to go, lean toward sharing.

Group Leadership Models

Lesson 1: Why Take the Fifth Step?

Relate that people who work Step 5 almost always report two things. Before they complete the Step, the person working the Step may say this Step is the most frightening thing they ever have undertaken. After they complete the Step, the person will say it is the most freeing thing he or she ever has done. Read the story of Jim's Step 5 on page 100 of the member's book. Tell about your struggle to share your Step 5 and about the benefits you have experienced by breaking the silence. Invite members to share their feelings about having taken or facing taking the Step.

On page 101 review the four statements that illustrate the benefits of confession. State the principle, "We are as sick as our secrets." Share something about the benefits you have experienced by sharing your fifth Step. Encourage members to share their feelings about Step 5.

Lesson 2: Taking the Step, Part I

Explain that shame is the feeling that we somehow are stained, evil, or wrong in a unique sense—that we are wrong in a way that others are not. On page 104 review the story of David's sin. State that since God forgave David, loved David, and even called David a man after His (God's) own heart, we can believe that God will forgive, love, and accept us as well. Share something about your experience in accepting the fact that God accepts you. Ask members to share how they feel about the matter of God's forgiveness and acceptance. Emphasize that feelings are feelings—sharing how you really feel is OK.

Explain that in our attempt to gain God's forgiveness, we often play a game of penance. Summarize the member's book section entitled "Accepting Forgiveness: Part of Confession" (page 105). Share something about your experience with making yourself do penance for your sin. Share how God is changing this habit as you work the Steps. Ask members to discuss how they relate to the concept of penance.

Lesson 3: Taking the Step, Part II

Summarize the member's book material about choosing a good listener (page 106). Relate that we usually best share Step 5 when we tell the story of our lives. Share something about the process you went through to prepare your fifth Step, enlist a listener, and share your confession. Emphasize that people have differing experiences with Step 5. Some people have an immediate feeling of great relief; others may not. The important issue is to break the bondage of secrecy that enables Satan to frighten us with the fear that our secrets will be disclosed and convince us that we're alone and helpless. Encourage members to tell their feelings about planning to take or having taken Step 5.

❖ *First Steps:* Freedom through Confession

Relate that people who work Step 5 almost always report two things. Before they complete the Step, people working the Step may say this Step is the most frightening thing they ever have undertaken. After they complete the Step, people will say the Step is the most freeing thing they ever have done. Read the story of Trish's Step 5 on page 25 of *First Steps*. Tell about your struggle to share your Step 5 and about the benefits you have experienced by breaking the silence. Invite members to share their feelings about having taken or about facing taking the Step.

Read the four "We will lose . . ." statements on page 25 of *First Steps*. State the principle, "We are as sick as our secrets." Share something about the benefits you have experienced by sharing your fifth Step. Encourage members to share their feelings about Step 5.

Explain that shame is the feeling that we somehow are stained, evil, or wrong in a unique sense—that we are wrong in a way that others are not. On page 26 of *First Steps* review the story of David's sin. State that since God forgave David, loved David, and even called David a man after His (God's) own heart, we can believe that God will forgive, love, and accept us as well. Share something about your experience in accepting the fact that God accepts you. Ask members to share how they feel about the matter of God's forgiveness and acceptance.

Summarize the member's book material about choosing a good listener (page 28 of *First Steps*). Relate that we usually best share Step 5 when we tell the story of our lives. Share something about the process you went through to prepare your fifth Step, enlist a listener, and share your confession. Emphasize that people have differing experiences with Step 5. Some people have an immediate feeling of great relief; others may not. The important issue is to break the bondage of secrecy that enables Satan to frighten us with the fear that our secrets will be disclosed and convince us that we're alone and helpless. Encourage members to tell their feelings about planning to take or having taken Step 5.

After the Meeting

❑ Read "Before the Meeting" for Step 6 on page 38 of the facilitator's guide to evaluate the amount of preparation you will need for your next group meeting. Record at the top of page 38 a time when you will prepare.

❑ Study carefully Step 6 and complete all the exercises in the *Conquering Chemical Dependency* member's book.

Acting in Faith

Step 6

We commit ourselves to God and desire that He remove patterns of sin from our lives.

Goals for Step 6

1. Recognize and surrender obstacles to your commitment to Christ.
2. Evaluate and choose six proper motivations for obedience.
3. Evaluate and choose to avoid four improper motivations for obedience.
4. Freely choose the role of a servant of the Lord Jesus Christ.

Before the Meeting

❑ Read and complete the learning activities for Step 6 in the *Conquering Chemical Dependency* member's book.
❑ Find a quiet time and place to pray for group members by name. Ask the Lord to give you the wisdom you need to prepare for and to lead the group meeting.
❑ Read the Group Leadership Models section which follows. The section provides activities that relate to each lesson in Step 6. Select the activities that best suit your group members' needs. Be aware that this section provides far more activities than you will have time to use during your meeting. Just as a reminder about which activities to choose, you likely will use only a few activities from this Step if you are using the 13-week overview schedule. If you use the Step Study schedule, you may use several of the activities before your group moves on to another Step. If you are following the traditional 12-Step format, the leader will select one topic from one of the examples given or from the leader's experience.
❑ Arrange the chairs in a circle.
❑ If you select an activity that involves a handout, make enough copies of the handout for each group member to have one.

Ask God to guide you as you seek a balance between providing activities while you allow enough time for spontaneous sharing. When you are in doubt about which direction to go, lean toward sharing.

Group Leadership Models

Lesson 1: Becoming Willing to Obey

Read or relate the first four paragraphs on page 113 of the member's book about the principle expressed in Step 6. Explain that as we desire what God desires, we will experience meaning and purpose in life. Remind group members that we seek progress rather than perfection in our application of the Steps.

Share some specific area of your life in which you have experienced progress in applying Step 6 to a problem. Invite group members to share their feelings and progress about Step 6.

On pages 115-117 of the member's book review the seven fears about God. Share your reaction about one or more of the fears and the progress you are making in replacing the fear. Ask group members to share about their fears.

Relate the story of Karen and the learning activity from Jeremiah 20 (page 116 of the member's book). Explain that many of us have the false belief that God cannot tolerate our anger, but the great leaders of the Bible honestly expressed their emotions to God. Share something about your journey to honestly face and express your anger to God. Encourage sharing.

Lesson 2: Positive Reasons to Obey

Make and distribute copies of Handout 9 (page 56 of the facilitator's guide). Briefly review the six positive reasons to obey God. Share your reaction to one or more of the reasons. Ask members to discuss their reactions and feelings about the list.

Lesson 3: Harmful Reasons to Obey

Briefly review the four harmful reasons for obedience (pages 121-123). Explain that these reasons result in unhealthy obedience. Share your experience with one or more of these reasons in your life and recovery. Ask members to share their experiences.

Lesson 4: Ownership and Conduct

From the lesson in the member's book (page 124) explain the principle of ownership. Share something about your journey to make the choice that Jesus Christ is the owner of your life. Invite group members to share their honest feelings and struggles about the issue of the lordship of Christ in their lives.

❖*First Steps* : Willing to Obey

Make and distribute copies of Handout 9 (page 56 of the facilitator's guide). Briefly review the six positive reasons to obey God. Share your reaction to one or more of the reasons. Ask members to discuss their reactions and feelings about the list.

Briefly review the four harmful reasons for obedience (pages 33-34 of *First Steps*). Explain that these reasons result in unhealthy obedience. Share your experience with one or more of these reasons in your life and recovery. Ask members to share their experiences in this area.

After the Meeting

❏ Read "Before the Meeting" for Step 7 on page 39 of the facilitator's guide to evaluate the amount of preparation you will need for your next group meeting. Record at the top of page 39 a time when you will prepare.

❏ Study carefully Step 7 and complete all the exercises in the *Conquering Chemical Dependency* member's book.

Ready for Change

Step 7

We humbly ask God to renew our minds so that our sinful patterns can be transformed into patterns of righteousness.

✧ Goals for Step 7

1. Identify why we need a renewed mind.
2. Determine the effect of performance-based worth on your life, and describe the solution.
3. Evaluate how addiction to approval affects your life, and describe the solution.
4. Estimate the effect of habitual blaming on your life, and describe the solution.
5. Estimate the effect of low self-esteem on your life, and describe the solution.
6. Describe three practical actions necessary to work Step 7.

Before the Meeting

❏ Read and complete the learning activities for Step 7 in the *Conquering Chemical Dependency* member's book.

❏ Find a quiet time and place to pray for group members by name. Ask the Lord to give you the wisdom you need to prepare for and to lead the group meeting.

❏ Read the Group Leadership Models section which follows. The section provides activities that relate to each lesson in Step 7. Select the activities that best suit your group members' needs.

❏ Arrange the chairs.

❏ If you select an activity that involves a handout, make enough copies of the handout for each group member to have one.

Group Leadership Models

Lesson 1: The Grace Step

Explain that depravity is the biblical teaching that sin has damaged every aspect of our lives (See page 128 of the member's book). Share some area of your life in which you have identified distorted thoughts, emotions, and behavior. Share how God is helping you to overcome and transform this sin damage as you continue to work your 12- Step program. Invite members to share how God is helping them to overcome denial; to see the results of depravity in their lives; and to change thoughts, feelings, and behaviors.

Explain the concept (page 130 of the member's book) that our belief system serves as a filter. We perceive the situations in our lives through the lenses of our belief system. Until we begin to make changes to our basic beliefs, we will have little success changing our thoughts, emotions, and actions. Share an example from your life in which you have identified one of the basic false beliefs that led to wrong thoughts, emotions, and behavior. Share what you are doing to replace the false belief with God's truth. Invite members to share how they see their belief system influencing and damaging their lives.

Lesson 2: The Performance Trap

Briefly summarize the member's book material about fear of failure. Make and distribute copies of Handout 10 (page 56 of the facilitator's guide). Share your response to the learning activity in the box on page 134, or share another example of a situation in which your performance did not measure up to the standard you set for yourself. Share how you identified the standard—part of your belief system—behind your response to the situation and behind your resulting thoughts, emotions, and actions. Emphasize how, by correcting the standard, you seek to respond in a more healthy and Christ-honoring way. Encourage group members to share their reactions to the handout. Ask them specifically to discuss how they react to the patterns they see working in their emotions and actions.

Read on page 135 about justification and explain this concept. Share with group members the following story someone in a group told: "I grew up in a church which taught that if you sinned, God would erase your name from the 'Lamb's Book of Life' and that you would have to be saved all over again. I had a dream one night that I saw the 'Book of Life' and saw that on my page, my name had been erased so many times that only a hole remained." Explain that the truth of justification is that God makes us just as if we never had sinned, and He views us as holy and righteous through Jesus. Share something about your journey to accept the fact that God has forgiven you and accepts you. Ask members to share about their journeys in this area.

Lesson 3: The Approval Addict

Summarize the member's book material about the false belief that *I must have the approval of certain others to feel good about myself.* Share something about your struggle with approval-based self-worth. Ask members to share their own struggles with this issue.

Read the four paragraphs under "God's Answer: Reconciliation" (page 139). Explain that when we have failed or someone disapproves of us, we can learn to use the following formula: "It would be nice if _____ (my boss liked me, I could fix the refrigerator, my complexion were clear, James had picked me up on time, or_____), but I'm still deeply loved, completely forgiven, fully pleasing, totally accepted and complete in Christ." Share an example from your life and recovery. Encourage members to share their reactions about this formula.

Lesson 4: The Blame Game

Briefly summarize the member's book section on page 143 under the subheading "The Fear of Punishment and the Tendency to Punish Others." Explain that this false belief leads to denial, the central characteristic of all addiction. The fear of blame keeps us from facing and changing our behaviors. Share an area of your life in which the fear of punishment kept you in bondage. Then share how the principle of propitiation sets you free from the fear of punishment. Ask other group members to tell their responses about the principle.

Lesson 5: Shame

Explain that the first three false beliefs lead to the final false belief—*I am what I am. I cannot change. I am hopeless.* In the past when we have experienced shame from other people, we often begin to shame ourselves. On page 148 of the member's book read the two

paragraphs under the heading "Shame and Performance." Share your response to the learning activity in which you described a time when you have acted in ways that illustrated your low self-worth or a time when you abused yourself. Encourage members to share how shame has impacted their self-worth and their performance.

On page 149 read the section under the heading "Shame and Appearance." Explain that God's answer to shame is the principle of regeneration. Share your reaction to the truth that God has made you new and complete in Christ. Ask others to share how they react to this truth.

Lesson 6: Taking the Step

Explain the process of making a truth card to create new patterns of thinking, feeling, and acting. Share the illustration of the ravine (page 151). Share your experience with the Truth Card and with creating new patterns. Encourage sharing.

Read the paragraphs under the heading "Exposing Ungodly Thoughts" (page 152). Share your responses to the learning activity in which you wrote your thoughts about the four basic truths. Emphasize to group members that God wants us to be honest. He understands when we react with skepticism to these changes in our old beliefs. Read the paragraph under the heading "The Awkwardness of Change" (page 154). Encourage group members to tell their reactions to one or more of the beliefs.

❖ *First Steps:* The Grace Step

Briefly review from *First Steps* one of the four false beliefs (The Performance Trap, page 35; The Approval Addict, page 36; The Blame Game, page 38; or Shame, page 39) and explain the corresponding truth from God's Word. Share your experience with replacing the false belief. Invite sharing.

After the Meeting

❑ Read "Before the Meeting" for Step 8 on page 42 of the facilitator's guide to evaluate the amount of preparation you will need for your next group meeting. Record at the top of page 42 a time when you will prepare.
❑ Study carefully Step 8 and complete all the exercises in the *Conquering Chemical Dependency* member's book.

Forgiveness and Amends

Step 8

We make a list of all persons who have hurt us and choose to forgive them. We also make a list of all persons we have harmed and become willing to make amends to them all.

✧ Goals for Step 8

1. Describe the nature of genuine forgiveness.
2. Describe six negative results of lack of forgiveness.
3. Describe four parts of the process of forgiving.
4. Make a list of the people you have harmed.

Before the Meeting

❏ Read and complete the learning activities for Step 8 in the *Conquering Chemical Dependency* member's book.

❏ Find a quiet time and place to pray for group members by name. Ask the Lord to give you the wisdom you need to prepare for and to lead the group meeting.

❏ Read the Group Leadership Models section which follows. The section provides activities that relate to each lesson in Step 8. Select the activities that best suit your group members' needs. Be aware that this section provides far more activities than you will have time to use during your meeting. Just as a reminder about which activities to choose, you likely will use only a few activities from this Step if you are using the 13-week overview schedule. If you use the Step Study schedule, you may use several of the activities before your group moves on to another Step. If you are following the traditional 12-Step format, the leader will select for the meeting one topic from one of the examples given or from the leader's experience.

❏ Arrange the chairs.

❏ If you select an activity that involves a handout, make enough copies of the handout for each group member to have one.

Ask God to guide you as you seek a balance between providing activities while you allow enough time for spontaneous sharing. When you are in doubt about which direction to go, lean toward sharing.

Group Leadership Models

Lesson 1: Persons to Forgive

Read the first two paragraphs of lesson 1 on page 157 of the member's book. Discuss the statement, "Stress makes us hug our addictions." Explain that the statement reminds us that when we begin to experience stress—such as stress brought on by lack of forgiveness—we are in danger of having old habits overcome us. Share an example of a time when you have experienced a "slip"—a time of returning to using—because of stress from guilt or unforgiveness. Ask group members to share about times that they have experienced this situation.

On page 157 read the five methods we often substitute for forgiveness. Explain that each of these methods fails to solve problems and falls short of genuine forgiveness. Summarize from the member's book the harmful results of failing to forgive. Share one or more examples of times when you have used these ineffective substitutes for forgiving. Encourage group members to share about times this has happened to them.

Tell the story of the unmerciful servant (page 159). Explain that having been forgiven motivates us to forgive others. Share about a time in your recovery when God's forgiveness motivated you to forgive someone else. Invite sharing.

Lesson 2: Forgiving Others

Make and distribute copies of Handout 11, Reasons We Don't Forgive (page 57 of the facilitator's guide). Share your reaction to one or more of the reasons and examples. Encourage group members to discuss which of the reasons they have used to avoid forgiving.

Summarize the six results of lack of forgiveness (pages 162-163 of the member's book). Share how lack of forgiveness has affected your life. Share how you have benefited from working this Step. Encourage group members to tell their experiences in this area.

Lesson 3: Taking the Step, Part 1

Explain that forgiveness is not erasure. Forgiveness is counting the debt paid in full. Read or summarize the discussion of forgiveness based on Christ's sacrifice (page 165). Share an example of your experience of learning to forgive. Invite others to share their examples.

Summarize the four-part process of forgiving described on page 166. Explain that we describe the person to be forgiven, the offense, the date, and the reasons for not forgiving. Share an example from your book of forgiveness. Ask group members to share examples.

Lesson 4: Taking the Step, Part 2

Read the list of questions to ask when you fill out your list of offenses (See page 167 of the member's book). Share something about your struggle to fill out your list and about the benefits you have experienced from the Step. Ask group members to share their experiences in this area.

❖ *First Steps:* Forgiveness and Amends

Make and distribute copies of Handout 11, Reasons We Don't Forgive (page 57 of the facilitator's guide). Share your reaction to one or more of the reasons and examples. Encourage group members to discuss which of the reasons they have used to avoid forgiving.

Read the list of questions to ask when you fill out your list of offenses (See page 44 of *First Steps*). Share something about your struggle to fill out your list and about the benefits you have experienced from the Step. Ask group members to share their experiences.

After the Meeting

❑ Read "Before the Meeting" for Step 9 on page 44 of the facilitator's guide to evaluate the amount of preparation you will need for your next group meeting. Record at the top of page 44 a time when you will prepare.
❑ Study carefully Step 9 and complete all the exercises in the *Conquering Chemical Dependency* member's book.

Making My Amends

Step 9

We make direct amends to people where possible, except when doing so will injure them or others.

 Goals for Step 9

1. Describe some of the benefits that come from making amends.
2. Identify four principles to guide confrontation.
3. Make your amends.

Before the Meeting

❏ Read and complete the learning activities for Step 9 in the *Conquering Chemical Dependency* member's book.

❏ Find a quiet time and place to pray for group members by name. Ask the Lord to give you the wisdom you need to prepare for and to lead the group meeting.

❏ Read the Group Leadership Models section which follows. The section provides activities that relate to each lesson in Step 9. Select the activities that best suit your group members' needs. Be aware that this section provides far more activities than you will have time to use during your meeting. Just as a reminder about which activities to choose, you likely will use only a few activities from this Step if you are using the 13-week overview schedule. If you use the Step Study schedule, you may use several of the activities before your group moves on to another Step. If you are following the traditional 12-Step format, the leader will select one topic from one of the examples given or from the leader's experience.

❏ Arrange the chairs.

❏ Copy handouts for members if necessary.

Group Leadership Models

Lesson 1: The Benefits of Amends

Read the first three paragraphs of the lesson from the member's book (page 171). Share the story of an amend you have made. Share your struggle to make the amend, your decision to do so, and the results of the amend. Invite group members to share which benefits of making their amends they most desire.

Lesson 2: The Mechanics of Amends

Briefly explain the three principal types of amends—direct amends, indirect amends, and delayed amends. Share from your life and recovery an example of one or more types of amends. Be particularly sensitive to avoid boasting about your amend or blaming the other person. Humbly and honestly share your struggle to make and benefit from having made the amend. Invite group members to share an amend they need to make or their feeling about making amends.

Lesson 3: Taking the Step

State that we usually accomplish or fail to accomplish our goals based upon our planning. Carefully selecting the people and writing the actions necessary for our amends prepares us to complete the task. Share about a time when you made a difficult amend. Encourage group members to share.

❖ *First Steps*: Making Amends

If you are facilitating a *First Steps* group, you may adapt and use any of the group leadership models above for this Step.

After the Meeting

❏ Read "Before the Meeting" for Step 10 on page 45 of the facilitator's guide to evaluate the amount of preparation you will need for your next group meeting. Record at the top of page 45 a time when you will prepare.

❏ Study carefully Step 10 and complete all the exercises in the *Conquering Chemical Dependency* member's book.

Recognizing and Responding

Step 10

We continue to take personal inventory, and when we are wrong, promptly admit it.

◇ **Goals for Step 10**

1. Distinguish between guilt and godly sorrow.
2. Identify ways that conviction and guilt occur in our lives and how they affect us.
3. Develop the skill of identifying false beliefs.
4. Practice identifying the warning signals of harmful behavior.

Before the Meeting

❑ Read and complete the learning activities for Step 10 in the *Conquering Chemical Dependency* member's book.
❑ Find a quiet time and place to pray for group members by name. Ask the Lord to give you the wisdom you need to prepare for and to lead the group meeting.
❑ Read the Group Leadership Models section which follows. The section provides activities that relate to each lesson in Step 10. Select the activities that best suit your group members' needs. Be aware that this section provides far more activities than you will have time to use during your meeting. Just as a reminder about which activities to choose, you likely will use only a few activities from this Step if you are using the 13-week overview schedule. If you use the Step Study schedule, you may use several of the activities before your group moves on to another Step. If you are following the traditional 12-Step format, the leader will select for the meeting one topic from one of the examples given or from the leader's experience.
❑ Arrange the chairs.
❑ If you select an activity that involves a handout, make enough copies of the handout for each group member to have one.

Ask God to guide you as you seek a balance between providing activities while you allow enough time for spontaneous sharing. When you are in doubt about which direction to go, lean toward sharing.

Group Leadership Models

Lesson 1: Guilt: A Devastating Burden

Read the first two paragraphs of the lesson from page 180 of the member's book. Share your response to the learning activity by sharing which Steps you are practicing with reasonable—not perfect—consistency and which Steps continue to cause you to struggle. Ask group members to tell how they see themselves growing in working the Steps.

Read the two paragraphs on page 182 under the heading "What Guilt Does to Us." Share your responses to the learning activity. Invite group members to share an incident and the destructive effect of guilt on their lives.

Read the two paragraphs at the top of page 183 under the heading "Recognize the Lies." Share a time when conviction caused you to experience godly sorrow for a sin. Invite group members to share.

Lesson 2: More About the Process

Make and distribute copies of Handout 12 on page 57. Read to the group the first two paragraphs of the lesson from pages 183 and 184. Briefly explain the chart. Share your reaction to the truths about guilt from the chart. Share something about your experience with guilt. Invite group members to share their reaction to the chart and/or their experience with guilt.

Lesson 3: Identifying False Beliefs

Briefly explain the process of tracing emotions to root beliefs (page 185-186). Share your answer to the learning activity on page 186. Invite group members to think of an occasion when they have experienced strong painful emotions—possibly leading to destructive behavior. Ask them to trace the strong emotion back to the root belief. Invite sharing. After sharing you may choose to read the paragraphs on page 186 under the heading "Learned Habits We Can Overcome."

Lesson 4: Catching the Signals

Briefly explain the test for a wise person from Proverbs 9:8 (page 187). Explain that for those of us who are irresponsible, the struggle is to honestly accept responsibility for our actions. For those of us who are *blame sponges*, the struggle is to see ourselves more objectively by refusing to accept inappropriate blame. Share an occasion when you have experienced correction. Share how you have struggled to take the correction and apply it to your life. Invite group members to share how they struggle to see themselves objectively.

Summarize the material from page 189 that deals with extreme thinking. Share an example from your experience in which you used the chart on page 190. Invite group members to share.

❖ *First Steps*: **Staying in Shape**

Briefly explain the process of tracing emotions to root beliefs (page 50-51 of *First Steps*). Share your answer to the learning activity on page 51. Invite group members to think of an occasion when they have experienced strong painful emotions which possibly led to destructive behavior. Ask them to trace the strong emotion back to the root belief. Invite sharing.

Summarize the material about dealing with distressing or painful emotions. Briefly explain the process of identifying, detaching, and deciding. Share a personal example in which you have used the method. Ask group members to share their examples.

After the Meeting

❑ Read "Before the Meeting" for Step 11 on page 47 of the facilitator's guide to evaluate the amount of preparation you will need for your next group meeting. Record at the top of page 47 a time when you will prepare.
❑ Study carefully Step 11 and complete all the exercises in the *Conquering Chemical Dependency* member's book.

A Growing Relationship

Step 11

We seek to know Christ more intimately through prayer and meditation, praying only for knowledge of His will and the power to carry that out.

◇ **Goals for Step 11**

1. Identify the primary purpose of prayer.
2. Describe Christian meditation.
3. Examine methods to help you work Step 11.

Before the Meeting

❑ Read and complete the learning activities for Step 11 in the *Conquering Chemical Dependency* member's book.

❑ Find a quiet time and place to pray for group members by name. Ask the Lord to give you the wisdom you need to prepare for and to lead the group meeting.

❑ Read the Group Leadership Models section which follows. Select the activities that best suit your group members' needs. Be aware that this section provides far more activities than you will have time to use during your meeting. Refer to "Before the Meeting" on page 45 of the facilitator's guide if you need a reminder about how to use these leadership models on the basis of which format your group is using to study this Step.

❑ Arrange the chairs.

❑ If you select an activity that involves a handout, make enough copies of the handout for each group member to have one.

Group Leadership Models

Lesson 1: What Is Prayer?

Read the paragraph titled "Praise" on page 194 of the member's book. Explain that humility is an accurate evaluation of ourselves. Emphasize that we need the humility that occurs when we acknowledge God as God. Share how praising God helps you to grow.

Invite group members to share how they feel about a growing humility and about praising God.

Summarize the section entitled "Sample Prayers" on page 196. Share how praying for a knowledge of God's will and the ability to obey His will has been important in your recovery. Invite sharing.

Lesson 2: Meditation

Explain that Christian meditation is different from Eastern meditation. The meditation of the Eastern religions relies on emptying the mind of conscious thought. Christian meditation is the discipline of growing in your knowledge of God by contemplating the Bible and the attributes or the acts of God.

Lesson 3: God's Word and Obedience

Explain that the purpose of Bible study is application —that we apply the truth of the Bible to change our lives. Share about a time when the Holy Spirit has convicted you through the Bible of a specific change needed in your life. Encourage group members to tell about times when the Bible has prompted them to change.

❖ *First Steps*: A Growing Relationship

If you are facilitating a *First Steps* group, you may use any of the group leadership models from lesson 1 or lesson 2 above.

After the Meeting

❑ Read "Before the Meeting" for Step 12 on page 48 of the facilitator's guide to evaluate the amount of preparation you will need for your next group meeting. Record at the top of page 48 a time when you will prepare.

❑ Study carefully Step 12 and complete all the exercises in the *Conquering Chemical Dependency* member's book.

4

Assisting Others

Step 12

Having had a spiritual awakening, we try to carry the message of Christ's grace and restoration power to others who are chemically dependent and to practice these principles in every aspect of our lives.

◇ **Goals for Step 12**

1. Describe two types of spiritual transformation.
2. Prepare to share your recovery testimony and your testimony of faith.
3. Practice applying the Steps to a life situation.
4. Identify resources for continued growth.

Before the Meeting

❏ Read and complete the learning activities for Step 12 in the *Conquering Chemical Dependency* member's book.

❏ Find a quiet time and place to pray for group members by name. Ask the Lord to give you the wisdom you need to prepare for and to lead the group meeting.

❏ Read the Group Leadership Models section which follows. The section provides activities that relate to each lesson in Step 12. Select the activities that best suit your group members' needs. Be aware that this section provides far more activities than you will have time to use during your meeting. Just as a reminder about which activities to choose, you likely will use only a few activities from this Step if you are using the 13-week overview schedule. If you use the Step Study schedule, you may use several of the activities before your group moves on to another Step. If you are following the traditional 12-Step format, the leader will select one topic from one of the examples given or from the leader's experience.

Group Leadership Models

Lesson 1: A Spiritual Awakening

Read or tell the story entitled "No Second-Class Believers" from the unit page of the member's book.

Share your experience of feeling like a second-class believer and how you related to Denise's story. Ask members to share their feelings about how they related to the story.

Explain the two models for spiritual transformation (page 207). Emphasize that neither model is superior to the other. Share which model is more nearly like your experience. Invite members to describe their spiritual experiences, spiritual awakenings, or where they are in relation to Step 12.

Lesson 2: Sharing the Message

Read page 210 in the member's book and explain the outline for sharing your recovery testimony. Emphasize that the outline is only an aid to organize and explain your experience. Use the outline to share your recovery testimony as you would when you make a Step 12 call. (A twelfth Step call is when a person shares his or her testimony to intervene in another person's addiction.) Invite members to share something about their recovery testimony or to share where they would like to be in their recovery.

Explain the four-part outline for sharing your Christian testimony from page 213 of the member's book. Use the outline to share your testimony of faith. Invite group members to share their testimonies of faith or to share where they would like to be in their relationship with God.

Lesson 3: Practicing the Principles

Read the story of "A Very Bad Day" from page 216. Share your responses to the exercises on page 217 about the story. Invite group members to share their insights and feelings about how the Steps can help them cope with difficult circumstances.

Lesson 4: Where Do I Go from Here?

Relate the story of "Denise, the Sponsor" from page 219. Explain that many of us complete our Step work and then feel that we need something to do next. Share about whether your experience parallels that of Denise. Share some things you have found to help you continue your spiritual growth. Encourage members to share some things they have found to continue their growth.

Some people may choose to go through the 12 Steps again for their personal development. Some may continue in a group because they sense that they can minister best by being sponsors or facilitators. Others need new material. Explain that at some point each person will complete the Steps. Although we never outgrow the Steps, nor do we stop doing the work of Step 12, we will arrive at the point of desiring additional growth. Summarize the final lesson in *Conquering Chemical Dependency* (page 219-221). Share ways you have found valuable to continue your spiritual growth. Invite sharing.

❖ *First Steps* : A Spiritual Awakening

If you are facilitating a *First Steps* group, you may use leadership models from the lessons above.

Briefly summarize and explain the information on page 59. Explain that the way we now deal with blame—by acknowledging our faults when appropriate and by refusing to accept the blame for others' actions—gives evidence of our spiritual awakening. Share your response to the learning activity on page 59. Encourage members to share.

Explain that we have the dual responsibility and privilege of sharing our faith and our recovery. Briefly share your recovery testimony and your faith testimony. Invite group members to share either their testimony of recovery, their testimony of faith, or their feelings about the Step.

Scriptures Related to the 12 Steps

Step 1

Psalm 5:1; 6:2-4,6-7; 10:14; 12:5; 13:1; 16:4; 18:6,27; 20:2-3; 25:16-18; 28:1-2; 30:10; 31:9-10,22; 34:18; 38:1-9; 39:4-5; 40:17; 42:6-8; 44:15-16; 51:17; 55:4-8; 69:1-3,20,33; 72:12-13; 88:1-4; 102:1-7; 116:1-9; 147:10-11; Proverbs 14:12; 18:14; 26:12; 28:26; Isaiah 55:8-9; Jeremiah 9:23-24; Matthew 9:36; Mark 4:35-41; Romans 7:18-20; 2 Corinthians 1:9; 3:4-5; 12:9-10; Ephesians 2:1-2; Hebrews 11:32-34; 1 Peter 2:9-10; 2 Peter 2:19

Step 2

Psalm 18:1-3,16-19; 20:7-8; 27:13-14; 33:18-22; 46:1-3; 71:1-3; 107:41-43; 109:21-27; 119:123-125; 119:162-166; 121:1-8; 130:1-8; 142:1-7; 149:4; Proverbs 1:7; 2:2-12, 15:16; Matthew 9:12-13; 12:18-21; 20:29-34; Mark 5:35-36; 9:23-24; Luke 1:37; 9:56; 11:5-13; 13:10-13; 18:35-43; John 3:14-18; 6:28-29,63,68-69; 7:37-39; 8:12; 10:9-10; 11:25-26; 12:46; 14:6; Acts 3:16; 4:12; 16:31; Romans 8:38-39; 1 Corinthians 1:18-25; 15:20-22; 2 Corinthians 1:8-11; 5:21; Galatians 1:4; Ephesians 2:4-5; Philippians 2:13; Colossians 2:13,14; Hebrews 2:14-18; 7:24-25

Step 3

Psalm 3:5-6; 4:8; 9:9-10; 17:6-8; 23:1-6; 28:6-9; 31:19-20; 56:3-4; 61:1-4; 62:5-7; 68:19:20; 86:11-13; 91:1-4; 94:17-19; 116:1-19; 143:8; 147:11; Proverbs 3:5-6; 14:26-27; Matthew 6:31-34; 10:37-39; 11:28-30; 16:21-26; Luke 9:57-62; 11:2-4; 24:46-47; John 1:12-13; 5:24; 6:35-40; 8:1-11; 12:26; 17:3; Acts 2:21; Romans 3:21-24; 4:20-25; 5:1,8-11; 8:1; 10:9-13; 2 Corinthians 1:3-5; Ephesians 1:3-14; 2:8-9; Hebrews 4:1-2; 1 Peter 1:3-5; 2:24-25

Step 4

Psalm 27:1-3, 13-14; 42:9-10; 51:6; 58:6-9; 66:18; 73:21-22; 90:8; Proverbs 5:3-6; 10:17; 13:13; 14:14-15; 15:11, 31-33; 16:2-3; 19:19; 20:1, 19-20; 21:9; 22:24-25; 23:27, 29-35; 25:28; 26:20-22; 29:20, 22-23; 30:11-12; Isaiah 26:3; Lamentations 3:40; Matthew 5:27-32; 10:8; 18:21-35; 23:23-28; Mark 11:25; Luke 7:36-50; 11:33-36; 12:1-6, 15-21; 16:14-15; 17:3-6; Romans 7:15; 12:3; 13:11-14; 1 Corinthians 3:1-3; 4:19-20; 7:3-16; 15:34; 2 Corinthians 6:14-7:1; 10:12; 13:5; Galatians 5:19-23; 6:3-5; Ephesians 4:1-3, 26-27; 5:18, 22-23; 6:1-4; Philippians 2:3-4; 4:5 -7; 1 Timothy 5:8; Hebrews 4:15 -16; 12:15; James 2:2-8; 1 John 1:5-10; 4:7, 11, 18

Step 5

Psalm 32:1-11; 38:18; 41:4; 51:3-4; 69:5; Proverbs 16:18; 21:2; 27:17; 28:13-14; Matthew 23:12; Luke 15:4-7; John 14:16-17,26; 16:13; Acts 19:18; Ephesians 4:14-15,25; Colossians 3:9; Hebrews 4:14-16; James 5:16; 1 John 1:9

Step 6

Exodus 21:1-2,5-6; Deuteronomy 5:29; 6:24; Psalm 4:3-5; 16:7; 19:7-14; 32:6-11; 94:12-13; 119:9-12,29-40; 139:23-24; 141:3-4; Proverbs 3:11-12; 13:18; 17:10; Matthew 3:8; 5:3; 7:24- 27; John 14:15,21; Romans 6:1-4,11-12; 12 : 2 ; 2 Corinthians 5:17; 7:9-10; Galatians 5:16-17; Ephesians 4:22; James 1:5-6

Step 7

Psalm 10:17; 25:8-11; 32:1,6-8; 34:4-6,15; 37:4-6,23-24; 39:7-8; 51:1-2,10; 79:9; 91;14-16; 103:2-5; 119:133; Proverbs 18:12; 22:4; Matthew 7:7-11; 15:22-28; 18:4; 21:21- 22; Luke 18:9-14; Acts 3:19; Romans 5:1; 12:2; 2 Corinthians 5:21; Philippians 4:19; Colossians 1:21-22; James 4:6; 1 Peter 5:6-7; 1 John 3:22-24; 5:14-15

Step 8

Proverbs 10:12; 14:1,30; Matthew 5:43-48; 6:14-15; 7:1-5; 18:21-35; 22: 36-40; Mark 11:25; Luke 6:31,37-38; 10:25-37; 19:8; John 13:34-35; Romans 2:1; 12;9,14,17; 13:8-10; 14:7-10; 1 Corinthians 4:5; 13:1-5; 2 Corinthians 5:9; Galatians 1:10; Philippians 2:3-4; 4:5,8; 1 Thessalonians 3:12-13; 2 Timothy 1;7; James 4:11-12; 5:9; 2 Peter 2:19-23; 3:8-12; 1 John 2:9-11; 4:19-21

Step 9

Psalm 51:14-17; 90:17; 126:5-6; Proverbs 3:27; 12:18-20; 15:1-4; 16:6-7,20-24; 25:11; Ezekiel 33:15; Matthew 5:9,23-24; 7:12; 12:35-37; Luke 6:27-36; Romans 12:18-21; 14:19; 15:2; 15:5-7; 1 Corinthians 8:1-3; Galatians 6:7-10; Philippians 1:9-11; 4:2; Colossians 3:12-13,18-21; 4:5-6; Philemon 8-17; James 3:17-18; 1 Peter 1:22; 1 John 3:17-19

Step 10

Psalm 24:3-5; 68:5-6; 85:8-9; 101:2-4; 103:8-18; Matthew 5:8; 12:34; 26:71-75; Luke 6:41-42; 14:25-35; John 17:15-17; Romans 8:1,13; 12:3,16; 16;19-20; 1 Corinthians 10:12-13,23-24; 2 Corinthians 5:15; 10:17-18; Galatians 4:9; 5:11,13-16; Philippians 2:14-15; James 1:13-14,19; 1 Peter 2:11; 3:17-18; 1 John 2:3,15-17

Step 11

1 Chronicles 16:11; 2 Chronicles 7:14; Psalm 1:1-3; 5:3; 50:15; 55:22; 66:16-20; 84:5-12; 105:1-4; 127:1-2; Isaiah 59:1-2; Jeremiah 29:11-14; 33:2-3; Matthew 5:6,23-24; 6:5-15; Mark 1:34-35; 6:45-46; Luke 3:21-22; 6:12-13,46-49; 9:28-31; 12:27-34; 22:39-46; John 3:30; 4:13-14; 8:31-32; 14:12-21; 15:4-11; 16:23-27; Acts 20:28-32; Romans 5:3-5; 8:26-28; 12:10-13; 1 Corinthians 10:31; 14:20; 15:58; 2 Corinthians 3:17-18; 5:14-15; 7:9-10; 9:6-15; Galatians 2:20; 5:22-26; 6:14; Ephesians 1:17-19; 2:18; 5:19-21; 6:10-18; Colossians 2:6-10; 3:14-17; 4:2; 1 Thessalonians 5:17; 1 Timothy 2:1-4; 2 Timothy 1:12-14; 2:15; 3:14-17; James 1:5-6,22-27; 1 Peter 1:20-21; 3:12; 4:7-11; 5:8-10; 2 Peter 1:2-8; 1 John 1:7; 4:9-10,19; 5:4-5,18-21

Step 12

Psalm 22:22-24; 35:27-28; 40:1-10; 78:4; 92:1-4; 96:1-2; 103:6-14; 106:1-3: 107:1-9; 111:1-6; Matthew 5:14-16; 11:28-30; 16:15-17; 28:19-20; Mark 5:19; 16:15; Luke 5:27-29; 12:35-40; John 1:40-45; 4:34-36; 15:16; Acts 3:6; Romans 1:14-17; 10:1, 14-15; 1 Corinthians 9:22-27; 15:10; 16:9; 2 Corinthians 2:14-17; 4:1-2; 5:10-11, 18-20; Galatians 6:1-2; Ephesians 2:8-10; Philippians 1:6; Colossians 1:9-13, 27-29; 1 Thessalonians 1:2-4; 2:3-4, 10-12; 5:14; 1 Timothy 1:5, 12-16; Titus 2:7-8; Hebrews 10:24-25; James 5:7-8, 19-20; 1 Peter 2:9-10; 3:15-16

Handout 1   The Addiction Process

✎ **Read the following paragraph which describes the progress of addiction. Circle each word or phrase that describes something you have experienced or that describes a reason you continue using.**

When we become hooked, the benefits we gained from our early drug use begin to fade as the years pass. Even though the early rewards are gone, our drug of choice becomes a reward for diligent work, a remedy for anger, a means of controlling other people, a boost for our energy level, an escape from pain—even when it is the cause of the pain, a substitute for companionship, a self-prescribed treatment for depression. The habit becomes a need. As the need grows, our lives begin to crumble. The drug of choice no longer will bring a sense of freedom. Instead a sense of slavery, isolation, anxiety, fear, and shame grows. We may experience broken relationships, the loss of a job, financial failure, declining health, and deteriorating self-esteem. Sadly, we may be the last to see our addiction. Without help we probably will die.

Handout 2   Self-evaluation Checklist

✎ **Check the box beside each statement which describes your experience.**

❏ My drug use doesn't make me feel as good as it once did.
❏ When I have been working diligently, I reward myself with my drug.
❏ I sometimes use because I am angry.
❏ I sometimes use to cope with difficult people.
❏ I sometimes use as a "pick-me-up"—to boost my energy level.
❏ I sometimes use to escape pain.
❏ I sometimes use because I am lonely.
❏ I sometimes use because I am depressed.
❏ I sometimes experience blackouts—periods of memory loss.
❏ I sometimes feel that I need to use.
❏ I sometimes feel that my life is crumbling.
❏ I feel guilty for using.
❏ I have broken relationships because of my drug use.
❏ I think my self-esteem is lower now than it was when I began to use.
❏ My using has contributed to my loss of a job.
❏ My using is affecting my health negatively.
❏ I have tried to quit and then began using again.
❏ I sometimes feel shame because I can't quit.
❏ It takes more of the substance to give me a high than it once did.
❏ It takes less of the substance to "wipe me out" than it once did.

52

Handout 3   Progress of Addictions Chart

✎ **Read and examine carefully the following chart. Draw a line on the curve to show how far your addiction has progressed.**

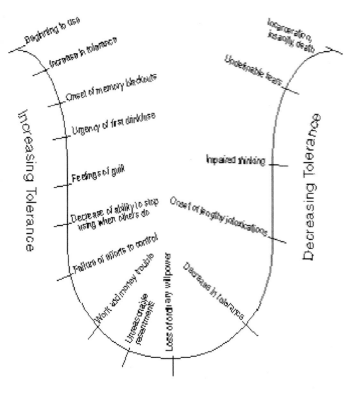

(Chart labels, reading down the left side of the curve):
Beginning to use
Increase in tolerance
Onset of memory blackouts
Urgency of first drink/use
Feelings of guilt
Decrease of ability to stop using when others do
Failure of efforts to control
Work and money trouble
Unreasonable resentment
Loss of ordinary willpower

(Left axis): Increasing Tolerance

(Chart labels, reading up the right side of the curve):
Incarceration, possibly death
Undefinable fears
Impaired thinking
Onset of lengthy intoxications
Decrease in tolerance

(Right axis): Decreasing Tolerance

Handout 4   The Stages of Addiction

Stage One: Experimenting and Learning
At this stage the user—

❑ typically uses "light stuff" (alcohol or marijuana), though occasionally may use hard drugs.

❑ experiences **euphoric** effects of alcohol or other drugs and suffers few consequences for using or drinking behavior.

❑ learns to trust the chemical substance and its effects and learns that the amount of intake controls those effects.

Stage Two: Seeking
Having learned that chemicals will produce "good" feelings, the user—

❑ establishes limits for using.

❑ usually can continue to control the amount he or she uses.

❑ may experience disruption in regular work or school activities.

❑ feels little emotional pain when choosing to drink or use.

Stage Three: Obsessing
Alcohol or other drugs become important. In this stage, the user—

❑ becomes preoccupied with getting "high."

❑ begins to experience periodic loss of control over use.

❑ loses sense of self-worth and instead begins to feel guilt and shame for behaviors when high.

❑ develops **ritualization**—a compulsive approach to using.

❑ begins to rationalize, to justify, or to minimize negative feelings about himself or herself.

Stage Four: Consuming
The substance "has" the user, and now he or she—

❑ must use just to feel "normal."

❑ believes other people and circumstances—never self—are the root of his or her problems.

❑ may entertain thoughts of suicide or running away.

❑ experiences deteriorating health and withdrawal symptoms.

❑ feels guilt, shame, remorse, anxiety, paranoia.

❑ experiences withdrawal symptoms.

Handout 5   Symptoms of Dependency

✎ **In the list of symptoms below, check those you have experienced.**

❑ Using a substance in larger amounts over a longer period of time than originally intended.

❑ Demonstrating an inability to reduce or control substance use, despite one's desire to stop or cut back.

❑ Spending large amounts of time in activities revolving around substance use. These activities can include planning, obtaining, using, and recuperating from the effects of use.

❑ Being intoxicated or suffering from withdrawal when you are expected to fulfill obligations at work, school, or home, or using in situations when substance use is hazardous to oneself and/or others, such as driving, piloting, operating machinery.

❑ Giving up or avoiding important social, occupational, or recreational activities to drink or use.

❑ Continuing to drink or use after recognizing that substance use is contributing to one's physical, psychological, relational, financial, occupational, or legal problems.

❑ Requiring increasingly larger amounts of the substance to achieve the desired effect.

❑ Experiencing withdrawal symptoms when you stop taking the substance or when you reduce your intake of it.

❑ Resuming or increasing substance use to relieve or avoid withdrawal symptoms — "eye openers."

Handout 6   Eleven Examples of Insanity

✎ **The following list contains examples of "insanity" — unsound judgment. Check every behavior that you have practiced. Add any additional examples in which you have participated.**

❑ 1. Drinking or using despite warnings of deteriorating health

❑ 2. Drinking or using despite the pain it causes others

❑ 3. Drinking or using in retaliation against someone who has offended us or made us angry — "I'll show you, I'll kill myself."

❑ 4. Drinking or using to prove we can "handle it," despite our experience that we can't

❑ 5. Getting close to success in any area of life, then "blowing it" with a binge

❑ 6. Changing or cancelling appointments or commitments to make time for using

❑ 7. Blaming other people for both our behavior and our inability to control our use of chemical substances

❑ 8. Insisting that we somehow are "different" from other people who are addicted to chemical substances

❑ 9. Drinking or using despite threats of loss — job, home, spouse — if we continue

❑ 10. Cutting ourselves off from friends, family members, or anyone else who attempts to interfere with our using

❑ 11. Drinking or using despite our earnest desire to stop

❑ 12. Others _____

_____

_____

Handout 7 — False Beliefs & God's Truths

False Beliefs	Painful Emotions	God's Truths
The Performance Trap: *I must meet certain standards to feel good about myself.*	**The fear of failure**	I am completely forgiven by and fully pleasing to God. I no longer have to fear failure. (Romans 5:1)
Approval Addict: *I must have the approval of certain others to feel good about myself.*	**The fear of rejection**	I am totally accepted by God. I no longer have to fear rejection. (Colossians 1:21-22)
The Blame Game: *Those who fail (including myself) are unworthy of love and deserve to be punished.*	**Guilt**	I am deeply loved by God. I no longer have to fear punishment or punish others. (1 John 2:2)
Shame: *I am what I am. I cannot change. I am hopeless.*	**Feelings of shame**	I have been made brand-new, complete in Christ. I no longer need to experience the pain of shame. (2 Corinthians 5:17)

Handout 8 — Self-pity Characteristics

Read carefully this list of common characteristics associated with self-pity. Check those you have thought, felt, or said.

❑ Projection: "I feel bad . . . it's your/his/her fault."

❑ Denial: "I never did anything wrong."

❑ Avoiding responsibility by reciting a long list of past hurts.

❑ Avoiding responsibility by pleading physical illness or distress.

❑ Reading the "whine list": "I can't." "I tried once before." "I never get anything right."

❑ Controlling others by making them feel important. "You're the only friend I have." "You're the only one who understands me."

Handout 9   Positive Reasons to Obey

1. Christ's love motivates us.
Our obedience to God expresses our love for Him.

2. Sin is destructive.
God's plans for my life always are for my good. Disobeying God always causes pain and hurt, although the pain may be delayed or disguised.

3. The Father's discipline trains us.
God is training me to live effectively and to obey Him for His glory and my good.

4. God's commands for us are good.
God gives commands to protect me from the harm of sin and to lead me to a life of effective service and victory.

5. God will reward our obedience.
My self-worth is not based on my performance and obedience, but my actions make a huge difference in the quality of my life and on my impact on others.

6. Christ is worthy.
Christ is worthy of my love and obedience.

Handout 10   Case in Point

Think of a situation in which your performance did not measure up to the standard you had set for yourself. Try to remember what thoughts and emotions arose because of that situation. What action did you take in response to those emotions? Read the example below; then write an example from your experience.

Situation: I failed to make a sale.
Standard: I must meet my quota to feel good about myself.
Thoughts: I'm a failure. I'll never make my quota. I'll never get promoted. I'll probably be fired any day now.
Emotions: Fear, anger, depression.
Actions: I avoided my boss for three days. I yelled at my wife and my kids. I took out my anger on them.

Situation: _____

_____

Standard: _____

_____

Thoughts: _____

_____

Emotions: _____

_____

Actions: _____

_____

1. The person never asked forgiveness.

2. The offense was too great.

3. The person won't accept responsibility.

4. I simply don't like the person.

5. The person did it too many times.

6. The person isn't truly sorry.

7. I've found an excuse for the offense.

8. Someone has to punish the person.

9. The person did it deliberately.

10. Something keeps me from forgiving.

11. If I forgive, I'll have to treat the offender well.

12. I'll forgive but I won't ever forget.

GUILT

Basic Focus — Guilt focuses on self-condemnation. We believe, "I am unworthy."

Primary Concern — Guilt deals with the sinner's loss of self-esteem and wounded self-pride. We think, "What will others think of me?"

Primary Fear — Guilt produces a fear of punishment. We believe, "Now I'm going to get it!"

Behavioral Results — Guilt leads to depression and more sin. We think, "I am just a low-down, dirty, rotten person." Or, it leads to rebellion. We believe, "I don't care; I'm going to do whatever I want to do."

Interpersonal Results — The interpersonal result of guilt is alienation, a feeling of shame that drives one away from the person wronged. We think, "I never can face him again."

Personal Results — Guilt ends in depression, bitterness, and self-pity. We think, "I'm just no good."

Remedy — The remedy for guilt is to remember that if you have repented of your sin, Christ has forgiven you and remembers your sin no more.

Welcome

We in this recovery group purpose to conquer the painful effects of chemical dependency. To that end we support each other as family. We seek to apply the biblical principles in the 12 Steps to our lives and to our relationships.

We welcome you. The only requirement for membership in this group is a desire to recover. We cannot fix your problems, and we will not seek to run your life for you. We will accept you and love you. This is a safe place.

We recommend several actions to help you begin recovery.

1. *Attend several group meetings before you decide if this is a group for you.*

2. *Read the information in this newcomer's packet. We also encourage you to obtain a copy of* Conquering Chemical Dependency: A Christ-Centered 12-Step Process *or* Conquering Chemical Dependency: First Steps to a Christ-Centered 12-Step Process, *begin to read the book, and complete the learning activities in the book. The book is available at the meeting, or members can tell you where you can get a copy.*

3. *Participation in the meetings is your choice. You can pass when it is your turn.*

4. *You will receive a phone list. Call a sponsor to work with you as you have questions and as you work on the Steps. Use the phone list to call people when you need help.*

5. *We guard the anonymity and confidences of group members carefully. Do not share who you see or what you hear in these meetings with any person or prayer list.*

6. *Keep coming back. God will change your life as you apply the Christ-centered 12 Steps.*

Attending this meeting is the first step in confronting the denial in our lives. We are glad that you are here, and we will encourage and support you as you grow with us.

_____

(group name)

Preamble

(to be read by the facilitator, group leader, or someone the facilitator or leader appoints)

We welcome you to the _____ (fill in group name) meeting of *Conquering Chemical Dependency*. This group is a fellowship of Christians who share our experiences, strength, and hope with each other so that we may solve our common problems and grow in Christ.

We recover by being honest with ourselves and others. We seek always to make this meeting a safe place, an affirming place, and a responsible place.[1]

- To make certain that this is a safe place, we keep everything said during this meeting confidential, and we keep it in this room.
- To make certain that this is an affirming place, we do not give advice. We desire to affirm that God can lead you to make healthy and Christ-honoring decisions. Please attempt to use "I" messages instead of "you" messages. We share our experience, strength, and hope.
- To make certain that this is a responsible place, we share only our own issues. We do not "take other people's inventories." We neither fix nor blame others. We seek to practice and model responsibility by allowing each other to be responsible for our own lives, decisions, and actions.

When we attended our first meeting, many of us were having a variety of feelings. We were relieved to find a place where people might understand our pain and despair. We were angry that we had to get help and could not manage alone this part of our lives. We felt lonely and were ashamed of the way our lives had become. We had secrets that we were reluctant to share.

Our group is not a therapy group or a study group. It is a Christ-centered support group. We do not give advice. We share our experience, strength, and hope with each other.

Here we learn a new way of living. We learn, at our own pace, to experience in a healthy way intimacy and sharing with others. We learn to trust, to ask for our needs to be met, to say no when no is appropriate, to express our feelings, and to hang around when all we want to do is run. Here no one shames us for what we have done or still are doing. Here we have a safe harbor within which to heal, and for that we are grateful. The only requirement for membership in our group is a desire to change our unhealthy behaviors.

Those of us who have experienced life change through the program need to challenge you. This program works as we complete the work with the help and supervision of a sponsor. If you do not have a sponsor, we encourage you to enlist one, complete the written work in the member's book, and share your work with your sponsor.

We are happy you are here. We encourage you to take one day at a time and keep coming back . . . it works.

(to be read by the facilitator)

My role is to guide our sharing. I may find it necessary to move the conversation in order that all may have time to share. We plan to close at , but in case our meeting runs over beyond this time, feel free to leave.

The Declaration

(This declaration of our identity in Christ is from *Search for Significance* LIFE Support Edition.)[2]

Because of Christ's redemption,
I am a new creation of infinite worth.

I am deeply loved,
I am completely forgiven,
I am fully pleasing,
I am totally accepted by God.
I am absolutely complete in Christ.

When my performance
reflects my new identity in Christ,
that reflection is dynamically unique.

There has never been another person
like me in the history of mankind,
nor will there ever be.
God has made me an original,
one of a kind, really somebody!

Notes
[1]Morris, Bill. *The Complete Handbook for Recovery Ministry in the Church* (Nashville: Thomas Nelson, Inc., 1993).
[2]McGee, Robert S. *Search for Significance* LIFE Support Edition (Houston: Rapha Publishing, 1992), 224.

The Twelve Steps of Alcoholics Anonymous*

1. We admitted we were powerless over alcohol—that our lives had become unmanageable.

2. Came to believe that a Power greater than ourselves could restore us to sanity.

3. Made a decision to turn our will and our lives over to the care of God *as we understood Him.*

4. Made a searching and fearless moral inventory of ourselves.

5. Admitted to God, to ourselves, and to another human being the exact nature of our wrongs.

6. Were entirely ready to have God remove all these defects of character.

7. Humbly asked Him to remove our shortcomings.

8. Made a list of all persons we had harmed, and became willing to make amends to them all.

9. Made direct amends to such people wherever possible, except when to do so would injure them or others.

10. Continued to take personal inventory and when we were wrong promptly admitted it.

11. Sought through prayer and meditation to improve our conscious contact with God *as we understood Him,* praying only for knowledge of His will for us and the power to carry that out.

12. Having had a spiritual awakening as the result of these steps, we tried to carry this message to alcoholics, and to practice these principles in all our affairs.

*From *Alcoholics Anonymous*, 3d ed. (New York: World Services, 1976), 59-60. The Twelve Steps are reprinted here and adapted on the following pages with permission of Alcoholics Anonymous World Services, Inc. Permission to adapt the Twelve Steps does not mean that AA has revised or approved the content of this workbook, nor that AA agrees with the views expressed herein. AA is a program of recovery from alcoholism. Use of the Twelve Steps in connection with programs and activities which are patterned after AA but which address other problems does not imply otherwise.

12 Traditions

Tradition One: Our common welfare should come first; personal recovery depends upon AA unity.

Tradition Two: For our group purpose there is but one ultimate authority—a loving God as He may express Himself in our group conscience. Our leaders are but trusted servants; they do not govern.

Tradition Three: The only requirement for AA membership is a desire to stop drinking.

Tradition Four: Each group should be autonomous except in matters affecting other groups or AA as a whole.

Tradition Five: Each group has but one primary purpose—to carry its message to the alcoholic who still suffers.

Tradition Six: An AA group ought never endorse, finance, or lend the AA name to any related facility or outside enterprise, lest problems of money, property and prestige divert us from our primary purpose.

Tradition Seven: Every AA group ought to be fully self-supporting, declining outside contributions.

Tradition Eight: Alcoholics Anonymous should remain forever non-professional, but our service centers may employ special workers.

Tradition Nine: AA, as such, ought never be organized; but we may create service boards or committees directly responsible to those they serve.

Tradition Ten: Alcoholics Anonymous has no opinion on outside issues; hence the AA name ought never be drawn into public controversy.

Tradition Eleven: Our public relations policy is based on attraction rather than promotion; we need always maintain personal anonymity at the level of press, radio, and films.

Tradition Twelve: Anonymity is the spiritual foundation of all our traditions, ever reminding us to place principles before personalities.

From *Twelve Steps and Twelve Traditions* (New York: World Services, 1981), 9-13.

The Christ-Centered 12 Steps for Chemical Dependency

Step 1
We admit that by ourselves we are powerless over chemical substances — that our lives have become unmanageable.

Step 2
We come to believe that God, through Jesus Christ, can restore us to sanity.

Step 3
We make a decision to turn our will and our lives over to God through Jesus Christ.

Step 4
We make a searching and fearless moral inventory of ourselves.

Step 5
We admit to God, to ourselves, and to another person the exact nature of our wrongs.

Step 6
We commit ourselves to God and desire that He remove patterns of sin from our lives.

Step 7
We humbly ask God to renew our minds so that our sinful patterns can be transformed into patterns of righteousness.

Step 8
We make a list of all persons who have hurt us and choose to forgive them. We also make a list of all persons we have harmed, and we become willing to make amends to them all.

Step 9
We make direct amends to such people where possible, except when doing so will injure them or others.

Step 10
We continue to take personal inventory, and when we are wrong, promptly admit it.

Step 11
We seek to know Christ more intimately through prayer and meditation, praying only for knowledge of His will and the power to carry that out.

Step 12
Having had a spiritual awakening, we try to carry the message of Christ's grace and restoration power to others who are chemically dependent and to practice these principles in every aspect of our lives.

Conquering Chemical Dependency Principles

These principles give the group a sense of purpose, direction, and focus. They remind the members of the group that the Lord is the ultimate source of healing and hope and that members can be patient and trusting in their healing process. The principles also explain many of the business aspects of the group. These principles are read at every group meeting in the Traditional Group Format, and they should be reviewed occasionally in the Optional Group Format.

Principle One
Our common welfare should come first: personal recovery depends upon the unity in Christ of all *Conquering Chemical Dependency* members.

Principle Two
We have but one ultimate authority—a loving God as shown to us through Jesus Christ. The Holy Spirit expresses Himself through our group as we share our experience, strength, and hope. Our leaders are trusted servants to the group.

Principle Three
The only requirement for group membership is a desire to change our chemically dependent behaviors.

Principle Four
The program is under the leadership of the local church which sponsors the group.

Principle Five
The primary purpose of the program is to carry the message of recovery to the chemical dependents. Groups never should endorse, finance, or lend the *Conquering Chemical Dependency* name to any related facility or outside enterprise because problems of money, property, and prestige may divert us from our primary purpose of helping other chemically dependent persons.

Principle Six
Each group should be self-supporting through collections participants take up in the meetings. The group declines outside contributions.

Principle Seven
The group should remain a non-professional organization. Where clerical or service help is needed, the group can pay people to provide these services. However, the group is free to anyone who wants to participate.

Principle Eight
The group has no opinion on outside social issues. This avoids having the name *Conquering Chemical Dependency* drawn into public controversy.

Principle Nine
The group's public relations policy is based on attraction rather than promotion. We maintain personal anonymity. Anonymity is crucial to the success of the group. It reminds us to place Christ and the principles of the 12 Steps before personalities.

The Steps of Recovery from Chemical Dependency

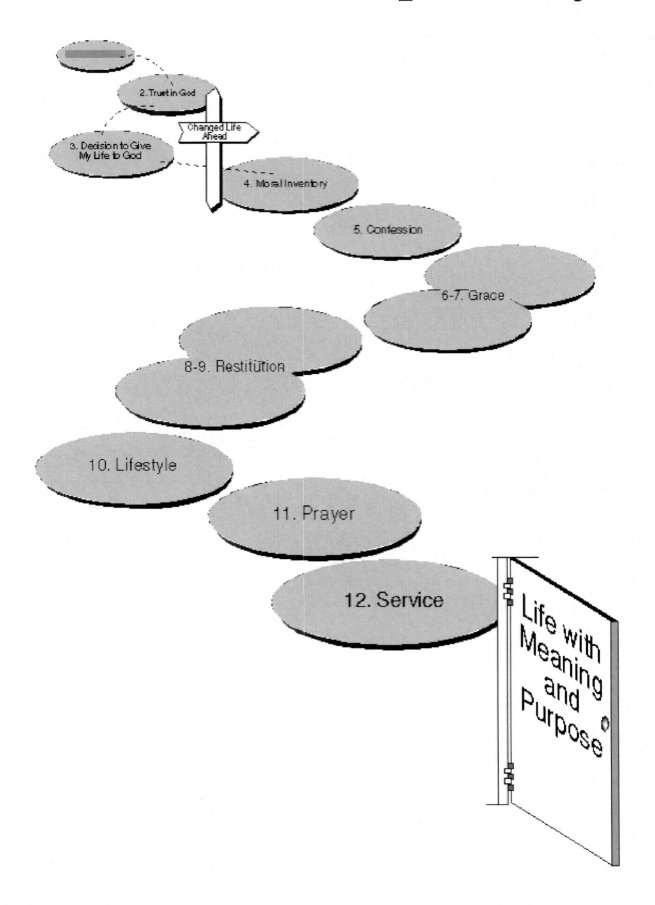

Made in United States
North Haven, CT
09 May 2024